# The Founding Fathers

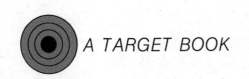A TARGET BOOK

# The Founding Fathers

Edited, with commentary by Bennett Wayne

GARRARD PUBLISHING COMPANY
CHAMPAIGN, ILLINOIS

**Acknowledgments:**

From *Old Ben Franklin's Philadelphia* by Elizabeth Rider Montgomery
(Champaign, Illinois: Garrard Publishing Company, 1967):
    "The General and Dr. Franklin"
    "A Walk in Freedom's City"
From *Mr. Jefferson's Washington* by Esther M. Douty
(Champaign, Illinois: Garrard Publishing Company, 1970):
    "Mr. Jefferson's Washington"

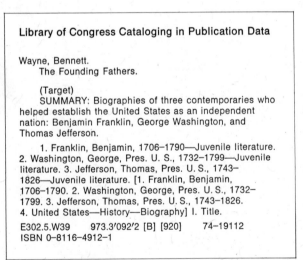

Library of Congress Cataloging in Publication Data

Wayne, Bennett.
    The Founding Fathers.

    (Target)
    SUMMARY: Biographies of three contemporaries who
helped establish the United States as an independent
nation: Benjamin Franklin, George Washington, and
Thomas Jefferson.

    1. Franklin, Benjamin, 1706–1790—Juvenile literature.
2. Washington, George, Pres. U. S., 1732–1799—Juvenile
literature. 3. Jefferson, Thomas, Pres. U. S., 1743–
1826—Juvenile literature. [1. Franklin, Benjamin,
1706–1790. 2. Washington, George, Pres. U. S., 1732–
1799. 3. Jefferson, Thomas, Pres. U. S., 1743–1826.
4. United States—History—Biography] I. Title.

E302.5.W39      973.3′092′2 [B] [920]      74–19112
ISBN 0–8116–4912–1

# Contents

# The Incredible Americans

It was a solemn moment for the assembly of merchants, planters, lawyers, and businessmen who were gathered in Philadelphia's State House that steamy day in July 1776. Young Thomas Jefferson, brilliant author of the Declaration of Independence, was presenting his history-making document to the Continental Congress.

Jefferson is seen in this painting flanked by the other members of his committee: Benjamin Franklin on his left, and John Adams, Roger Sherman, and Robert Livingston on his right. It is clear from the serious expressions on their faces that this was a fateful act. By accepting the Declaration, the Congress would defy both king and country. There was no return.

Who were these Founding Fathers—these men who had dared to gamble their all on a new nation? They were the citizens of a free society. They were a brand-new breed— Americans!

Together they would declare their right to govern themselves, fight a war against overwhelming odds, and bring forth an enduring constitution.

This book is about a few of these men: Benjamin Franklin, author, wit, inventor, and statesman, said to be "the most American of Americans"; George Washington, whose integrity and courage made him the undisputed leader of the fledgling nation; and Thomas Jefferson, distinguished lawyer, writer, statesman, and firm believer in human rights. These men were farseeing patriots and giants in an age of giants.

7

# Benjamin Franklin

## Spokesman for Democracy

### by Charles P. Graves

## 1. Candle Beams

Young Ben Franklin walked as quickly as he could through the narrow, cobbled streets of Boston. It was a hot summer day in 1718.

It had been fun swimming in the pond with Tom, but if he didn't hurry, Ben realized, he'd be late for dinner.

Ben grinned as he thought about his "swimming machine." The machine consisted of two foot-long wooden boards. Each one had a hole in the middle. Ben had put his thumbs through the holes and used the boards as paddles as he swam through the blue-green water of the pond. He had raced with Tom and won by ten yards!

The swimming machine was fun, but Ben had hundreds of other ideas he wanted to try. He sighed. There never seemed to be enough time!

As Ben neared his street he broke into a run. He slipped in the door just in time for supper. His mother had finished cooking the meal in the big fireplace. His father and his many brothers and sisters were sitting at the table.

Ben's father looked up. "Have you been wasting time again watching the ships come in?"

"Not today, father," Ben answered. "But watching ships isn't a waste of time! You know I want to be a sailor when I grow up. I want to go everywhere and see everything."

"No, Ben," Mr. Franklin said. "I have told you before. You have a good mind. I want you to have something better than a sailor's life. I am sorry I had to take you out of school. But I just did not have the money to keep you there."

Ben had been born in Massachusetts in 1706. Massachusetts belonged to England then. It was one of the young American colonies. There weren't many schools in the colonies, but Ben was luckier than most boys. He went to school for two years. After that he studied at home.

Ben also helped his father in his business. His father made candles to sell to the people of Boston. Ben heated the candle wax and poured it into the molds.

"I know you don't like working for me," Mr. Franklin once said to Ben. "Most boys don't like working for their fathers."

"It's not that," Ben said quickly. "I don't like making candles. I want to do something more important."

"You think making candles is not important?" Mr.

Young Franklin helped his father make candles for
the people of colonial Boston.

Franklin cried. "Without candles, how could people see at night? How could they read?"

He pointed to a candle burning brightly on a table. " 'How far that little candle throws his beams,' " he said proudly. " 'So shines a good deed in a naughty world.' "

"That's good, that's good!" Ben clapped his hands. "Did you make that up?"

"No. A famous writer named Shakespeare did."

"I wish I could write things like that," Ben said.

His father smiled. "You know, Ben, you have always been interested in words and ideas. You like to write. Perhaps you should be a printer. Your brother James may need a boy to help with his business."

"I think I would like printing, father," Ben said. "And I just had an idea. Making candles *is* important. If you don't keep on making candles, how can people read the things I'm going to print?"

"Well said, young man," his father cried. "We will go to see James tomorrow."

## 2. "Silence Dogood"

When Ben was growing up, boys learned a business by becoming apprentices. An apprentice agreed to work for a certain number of years without pay. In return, the man he worked for taught the boy a trade. An apprentice lived with his master and got free meals.

Mr. Franklin took Ben to see James at his printing shop.

"Good morning, James," Mr. Franklin said. "I wonder if you would hire Ben as an apprentice."

"I do need a boy," James answered, "but remember this. I won't be easy on Ben just because he is my brother."

"I don't want any favors," Ben said. "I want to learn to be a printer."

Ben promised to work for his brother until he was twenty-one. From the very first day, he liked the printing business. It was fun spelling out words with the metal letters, or type. And it was even more fun to ink the type and see the words printed on paper.

But James was not kind to Ben. He often scolded him. He was jealous because Ben learned so quickly.

James was pleased, however, when Ben thought of a money-saving idea. "Give me half the money you pay for my meals," Ben told James. "I will feed myself and you can save the rest."

Ben's idea made James happy. And Ben was happy too. He often made a whole meal out of a slice of bread and a handful of raisins. He spent only half the money James gave him for food. The

money he saved he spent on books. When Ben finished reading one book, he sold it. Then he bought
another book.

James printed a newspaper called *The New England
Courant*. One day Ben said, "James, I would like to
write a story for the newspaper."

James laughed. "You are much too young. Who
would want to read anything you wrote?"

Ben's feelings were hurt. He thought he was a
pretty good writer. He had a friend, John Collins,
who was an apprentice in a bookstore. Ben often
wrote stories and read them to John. John always
liked what Ben wrote.

"Why don't you play a trick on James?" John
suggested later. "Write a story and make James think
a grown-up wrote it."

"That's a good idea," Ben said. "And you know
how I like good ideas!"

There were no typewriters in those days. Everything had to be written by hand. Ben wrote a story,
but he changed his handwriting so James would not
know it was his. To fool James even more, he
signed the story "Silence Dogood."

Late that night Ben slipped the story under the
door of the printing shop. The next morning James
found the story.

"This is good," James shouted. "Mighty good! I

wonder who wrote it. I'm sure he must be an important man!"

Ben almost laughed out loud.

"Here, Ben," James said, handing him the story. "We will print this in the next copy of the *Courant*."

That was one copy Ben really enjoyed printing. When people read his story, they liked it and asked for more. So Ben kept on writing. The readers tried to guess who "Silence Dogood" really was. They knew it was a made-up name. But nobody guessed a boy like Ben could write so well.

One day Ben proudly told James that he was "Silence Dogood."

"You!" his brother cried. "I don't believe it. The stories are not written in your handwriting."

"I changed my writing so you wouldn't guess," Ben explained.

Then James knew that Ben was a better writer than he was. James was even more jealous than before. He did not like having such a smart younger brother.

James became harder and harder to work for. Nothing Ben did pleased him. James often became angry for no reason at all. He beat Ben with a stick. Ben decided he could not work for James any longer.

He knew he would have to leave Boston. He had promised to work for James until he was twenty-one.

This engraving from an old book shows Ben as a
young printer.

If he broke his word, James could keep him from getting another job in Boston. He might even have Ben arrested.

John Collins agreed to help Ben escape. He found a ship that was sailing for New York. Ben had to sell some of his precious books to pay for the trip. Late one night he crept onto the ship.

When Ben awoke the next morning, the ship was far out to sea. Ben was just seventeen. He had no friends in New York, and he had very little money in his pockets. But he had good ideas in his head. And good ideas are often worth lots of money.

## 3. On His Own

Ben could not find a printing job in New York. He soon found that he had almost no money left.

"Maybe I should go back home," he said to himself. But he knew he would feel like a failure if he did.

Someone told Ben he might find a printing job in Philadelphia. Ben thought his problems over carefully.

"What have I got to lose?" he laughed. He felt the few coins still in his pockets. Then he started for Philadelphia.

First he took a boat to New Jersey. Then he started hiking. He walked fifty miles in the rain.

When he reached the Delaware River, he found a rowboat that was going to Philadelphia. Ben climbed in and helped row.

Here is the way Ben described his arrival in the city where he was to become famous:

> I was dirty from my journey. My pockets were stuffed out with shirts and stockings. And I knew no soul nor where to look for lodging. I was fatigued with traveling, rowing and want of rest. I was very hungry and my whole stock of cash consisted of a Dutch dollar and about a shilling in copper.

Ben was so tired that he went into a church and fell asleep. When he awoke, he found a room at a hotel. Ben was hungry. He was glad when dinner was ready.

While he was eating, one of the men at his table asked, "Where are you from, young fellow?"

"Boston," Ben answered.

"What are you doing so far from home?"

Ben was upset. "This man may guess I'm a runaway apprentice," he thought. "He might send me home."

Ben knew he must say something quickly. "You

see, sir," he explained, "I learned the printing trade in Boston. But I couldn't get a job there or in New York. So I have come to Philadelphia to make my living."

The man seemed satisfied. "Well, good luck, my boy," he said. "I'm sure you will succeed."

The man was right. Ben got a job with a Philadelphia printer almost at once. The next few years were full of adventure. Ben took a trip on a sailing ship to London. He worked there as a printer for eighteen months.

When Ben returned to Philadelphia, he and a friend started their own printing shop. It was a great success. Ben also bought a newspaper. He made it the best paper in all the colonies.

Now that Ben was making money, he decided he should marry. "A single man," he thought, "is like the odd half of a pair of scissors."

When Ben first came to Philadelphia, he had met a girl named Deborah Read. He had been in love with her for a long time. Now at last he was able to marry her.

Deborah was a good wife. She made Ben's clothes. And she helped in the printing shop. She folded the pages and sewed them together to make books. Deborah helped Ben save money. He was proud of her.

Deborah was also busy taking care of the baby, William. When Francis was born, Ben and Deborah were happy with their growing family.

In those days many children died of smallpox. Deborah was planning to have Francis inoculated against the disease, but the doctor thought she should wait until Francis was stronger.

It was a terrible mistake. One night Deborah and Ben were awakened by loud crying. It was Francis. They felt his forehead. It was very hot. Ben went for the doctor, but it was too late. Francis had smallpox. In a few days he was dead.

Deborah and Ben were heartbroken. They didn't have another baby for many years. But when Sally arrived, she was a great joy.

The years flew by. Ben's days were crowded with his work and with dozens of other interests. He wrote his mother that when he died he wanted people to say that "he lived usefully" rather than "he died rich."

Ben certainly lived usefully, but his many good ideas were also making him rich.

## 4. Trying Everything

Benjamin Franklin made a success of nearly everything he tried—and he tried nearly everything. He published a yearly magazine called *Poor Richard's*

These scenes from *Poor Richard's Almanac* illustrated Ben's witty sayings.

*Almanac.* It contained something of interest to almost everyone. Farmers liked the weather reports. Sailors liked the news about the tides. Women read the cooking lessons. And children enjoyed the poems.

*Poor Richard's Almanac* became famous for the wise sayings in it. Among them were:

Eat to live; not live to eat.

Early to bed and early to rise makes a man healthy, wealthy and wise.

Ben made up some of the sayings himself. But he took most of them from the writings of other wise men. He often changed the words so people could understand them better.

Ben and some of his friends started a club called the Junto. The club members studied various topics and then discussed them at the meetings. This led to a lively exchange of ideas.

Because there were very few books in the colonies at that time, the members borrowed books from one another. They often found in these books new ideas to discuss.

One night Ben asked the club members a question. "If a king tries to take away the rights of a man, does the man have a right to resist?"

It was a hard question to answer. At that time the

colonies were ruled by the king of England. Many people thought a king could do no wrong.

Another member of the club stood up. "I think a man should fight for his rights," he said, "even if he has to fight a king."

"Before he fought," Ben said quietly, "wouldn't it be wiser to talk with the king? Even a king should listen to reason."

Ben did not know it at the time, but the question they were talking about would fill his thoughts for many years.

When the Junto meeting came to an end, Ben started for home. It was a dark night, and there were no street lights in Philadelphia.

As Ben was crossing a street, he tripped on a piece of firewood someone had dropped. Ben went sprawling into a mud puddle. His wife hardly recognized him when he reached home.

"It's me. Ben," he said, wiping the mud from his face.

"Your suit is ruined!" Deborah said.

"I'm lucky I didn't break my leg," Ben replied. "The streets are not safe at night. Something must be done."

Ben saw that something was done. He got Philadelphia to light the streets at night. And he arranged to have the streets swept clean. "Maybe it's

Benjamin Franklin as a fireman. The inventive Philadelphian started the city's first fire company.

a good thing for other people that I fell in that mud puddle!" he told Deborah.

And that wasn't all Ben did. He helped start the city's first fire department and the first hospital. He also helped set up in Philadelphia the first lending library in North America.

Ben was certainly busy. Yet when he had "time off," he invented things. One of his most famous inventions was the Franklin stove. In those days, there was no central heating. Houses were heated only by fireplaces, and too much of the fireplace heat went up the chimney. Ben hated to see his wife and children shivering, so he invented a stove which fitted in the fireplace. It sent heat out into the room. Soon many families had Franklin stoves to keep them warm.

Ben would not take any money for his invention of the stove. "I use inventions of men who lived before me," he explained. "Let other men use mine."

## 5. Ben Flies a Kite

When Ben was alive, electricity was a great mystery. No one knew much about it, but scientists all over the world were studying electricity. Ben was one of them.

Ben knew that lightning acted like electricity. But was it electricity? If Ben could only prove it! As usual, Ben had an idea. Perhaps he could prove that lightning was electricity by flying a kite during a thunderstorm. He knew that if lightning was electricity, it would travel down a wet kite string.

"William," he said to his son one summer day, "I want you to help me with an experiment. But we must keep it a secret. People will laugh at us if it doesn't work."

Ben and his son made a kite out of a big silk handkerchief. They attached a wire to the frame. Ben thought the wire would attract lightning.

Neither Ben nor William knew it, but the experiment was very dangerous. If a strong lightning bolt struck the kite, they could be killed.

One dark and stormy day they took their kite to a field. William held the ball of string attached to the kite. Ben held the kite. He flung it into the wind and yelled, "Go!"

William ran as fast as he could. At first, the kite wobbled from side to side. Then it rose gracefully into the air.

It was raining hard as Ben took the kite string from his son. They walked to a nearby shed. Ben tied a key to the end of the kite string.

The kite flew into a thundercloud. Lightning flashed, thunder roared, but nothing else happened.

"I'm afraid it's not going to work, father," William said.

"Let's not give up yet," Ben answered.

Lightning flashed again. Crack! It struck the wire on the kite frame.

Suddenly the tiny threads on the kite string stood up straight. They were moved by an unseen force. Ben touched the key with his hand.

"Ouch!" he howled, taking his hand away quickly. "I got a shock! But we've proved it! Lightning *is* electricity!" He was lucky that the lightning which struck the kite was weak and that he was not really hurt.

On their way home William said, "Now, father, we have proved that electricity and lightning are the same. But what good is it?"

Ben smiled. "Knowing the truth is always good. And I am sure something good will come of our experiment. Just you wait and see."

Ben was right. Soon he thought of a way to use his newly found knowledge. Lightning sometimes strikes houses. It can set them on fire. Ben invented a way to protect houses from this danger.

This fanciful painting of Ben Franklin's kite experiment decorated an early fire engine.

Ben told the readers of his almanac how to make lightning rods out of metal. He advised every man to put a rod on top of his house and connect the rod to the ground by a wire. When the lightning struck the metal rod, it would travel down the wire to the ground. The house would not be hurt. Lightning rods were put on many homes. Thanks to Ben, many lives were saved.

Ben's experiments with electricity were written about in Europe. He became famous all over the world. Many colleges gave him honorary degrees. From that time on, Ben was called "Doctor Franklin."

## 6. Ben Goes to England

Dr. Franklin was now the most important man in Pennsylvania. He was a member of the Pennsylvania Assembly. The assembly was a group of men who made laws for the colony. However, many laws for Pennsylvania were still made in England. They were made by the king and the English Parliament.

One night Franklin came home from an assembly meeting with exciting news.

"I must go to England very soon," he told Deborah and Sally.

"Oh, Ben," Deborah said, almost crying, "why must you go?"

"The assembly wants me to talk to the king and the members of Parliament. They don't seem to understand our problems."

"May mother and I go with you?" Sally asked.

"I hope so," her father answered. "William is too busy to come. I'd hate to go alone."

"No," Deborah said, "Sally and I must stay here. The trip is too dangerous."

Franklin thought he would be gone for only a few months. But he had to stay in England ten years.

While he was in England, Parliament passed a law called the Stamp Act. It forced Americans to pay special taxes on all legal papers, newspapers, and books. The Americans were very angry.

"We are willing to pay taxes," Franklin told the English. "But only if the taxes are fair. We must be allowed to make the tax laws ourselves. You live too far away. You don't know what is right for the colonies."

Franklin worked hard to get Parliament to end the Stamp Act.

"If the Stamp Act is not ended," he said, "Americans will stop buying English products. You will lose more money in trade than you would ever make in taxes."

The English knew he was telling the truth. Parliament repealed the Stamp Act.

Dr. Franklin playing chess with Lady Howe. The envoy from Philadelphia loved England, but he became convinced that the colonies must be free.

When the news reached Philadelphia, the people were happy. "Hurrah for Ben Franklin!" they shouted.

Sally was proud of her father. She wished he could come home. Sally had married William Bache, and she wanted her father to meet him.

However, Franklin had to stay where he was. The troubles with England got worse. Parliament passed still another tax law. This one made the Americans even more angry.

"Why can't the English and the Americans live in peace?" Franklin asked. "We can make our own laws. The English can make theirs."

But the king and Parliament wanted to make the laws for both. As Franklin had told the Junto Club years before, "Even a king should listen to reason." But King George III would not listen.

Franklin had done all he could. Just before he sailed for home, he had bad news from Philadelphia. His beloved Deborah was dead.

Franklin's homecoming was sad. But his heart filled with joy when he saw Sally and his two grandsons. Their names were William and Benjamin Bache.

"Here is an English penny for each of you," Franklin told his grandsons. "Promise that you won't spend them on English things!"

The boys were happy when their famous grandfather moved into their house to live.

## 7. A New Job

Fighting had broken out between England and the American colonies while Franklin was on the ship coming home. The American Revolution had begun.

Franklin had to go right to work to help the colonies plan the war. He was one of the leaders chosen to go to a meeting of the Continental Congress in Philadelphia.

At the meeting Franklin helped write the Declaration of Independence. It told the world that the American colonies were free and independent. No longer would they be ruled by unjust laws from England. The Declaration was passed on July 4, 1776.

When Franklin came home that night, he told his grandsons about the Declaration.

"It will mean a long war with England," Franklin explained.

"Are you going to be a soldier, grandfather?" Benny asked.

"I'm too old for that," Franklin answered, smiling.

But Franklin could help win the war in other ways. England was rich and powerful. The colonies were poor and weak. The American leaders knew they must get help from France if they were to defeat the English. And they knew that the man to send was Franklin. People would listen to his ideas.

Ben Franklin was on the committee chosen by the Congress to write a Declaration of Independence. He is seen here, seated in the foreground, in a thoughtful mood as the delegates begin to vote.

So once more Franklin sailed across the sea. His father had not let him be a sailor. But he was "going everywhere and seeing everything" just the same.

Franklin took two of his grandsons with him. Temple Franklin, William's son, was almost seventeen. Benjamin Franklin Bache was only seven. He had such a happy nature that he made his grandfather feel young again.

They sailed on the *Reprisal*. One day Benny stopped the captain on deck. "Captain," he asked, "what will happen if the English capture our ship? Temple says they might hang our grandfather."

The captain laughed. "First they will have to catch up with us," he said. "This is a fast ship. And even if they should catch up with us, we would probably capture them!"

He was right. The *Reprisal* captured two English ships and took them to France. They were prizes of war. It was an exciting adventure for the boys.

Soon after they arrived in France, they moved into a nice house near Paris. Temple became his grandfather's secretary and helped him with his work. Benny went to boarding school nearby.

Franklin soon became popular with the French people. His quick wit and friendly manner charmed them. The French liked his plain clothes and his old fur cap.

Plain Ben Franklin delighted the French with his brilliant mind and sharp wit. Detail from a painting by John Trumbull.

Sometimes Franklin was not well. He ached all over. So he would sit for hours in a bathtub of warm water, which made him feel better. But even when he felt sick, he kept on working. The bathtub had a cover on top. He asked important visitors to talk to him while he soaked in the bathtub!

And when he was well he went everywhere. The French people gave parties for him. Franklin was so popular that many families hung paintings of him in their homes. A picture of his face was put on medals and rings. Franklin wrote Sally that the pictures "have made your father's face as well known as that of the moon."

## 8. Winning the War

Franklin was very busy trying to get the French government to help the new nation. At first the French were afraid to send soldiers to America. If they did, England might make war on France.

"I'll never give up," he told Temple. "France must help us win our freedom from the English."

Finally, after years of hard work, Franklin was successful. France agreed to help America in its war with England.

King Louis XVI of France invited Franklin to a reception at his palace. The king was going to announce to the world that a treaty of friendship between the two countries had been signed.

Temple said his grandfather must wear a wig to the palace. In those days all important men wore fancy wigs over their own hair.

"But I don't own a wig," Franklin said.

"I thought you would say that," Temple answered, "so I had one made."

Temple reached in a box and pulled out a wig. Franklin tried it on, but the wig didn't fit.

"It's too little," Franklin said happily.

Just then a servant came into the room. "The wig is not too little, sir," he said. "Your head is much too big." He meant that Franklin's head was full of big ideas.

Franklin laughed. He went to the palace without a wig. Everyone who saw him said, "What a fine looking man!"

The king took Franklin by the hand. "I want you to tell the Americans how pleased I am with your work."

Even with French aid, the war went on and on. But one autumn day a ship from America brought wonderful news. American and French soldiers had captured the strongest English army in America. This meant the war would soon be over.

"Can't we go home now, grandfather?" Benny asked.

"Not yet," Franklin said, "there is still work to be done."

"You've done as much work as ten men!" Benny said.

"I will never be through working for my country," Franklin said. "We must stay in France until the peace treaty with England is signed."

When the peace treaty was finally signed, Franklin said, "I hope we never see another war! There never was a good war or a bad peace."

## 9. Waiting to Go Home

Before Franklin could go home, he had to wait for an American to take his place. Someone had to look after the new country's business in France.

During the years abroad, Franklin had never lost his

Dr. Franklin and his youngest grandson watched this famous balloon ascension at the Tuileries in 1783.

interest in science. He was still curious about everything. He did experiments whenever he had a chance.

Now all Paris was excited about a new invention. It was a huge balloon that could carry a big basket up in the air. A rooster, a sheep and a duck had been sent up in the basket. Now two brave men were going to try it. If they succeeded, they would be the first men to fly.

Franklin was as excited as the smallest boy. He took Benny out of school. They rode in a carriage to the park where the flight would take place.

The two brave men got into the basket. Other men untied the ropes that held the balloon down. What a thrilling sight it was when the balloon slowly rose in the air! The flyers waved. The people below all cheered.

"That's certainly better than any of my kites!" Franklin told Benny. "Perhaps the balloon will mean the end of war. Soldiers could be flown to enemy countries. Wars will get so terrible that maybe people will stop having them."

Franklin was enjoying his last years in Paris. He loved the French people, but still he longed to go home. He was old, and he was often sick. He wanted to see his family again.

At last, Thomas Jefferson arrived in Paris from America. He would work with Franklin to arrange trade treaties with European nations. In time he would take over Franklin's work. A Frenchman asked Jefferson, "Have you come to take Franklin's place?"

"I have come to succeed him," Jefferson answered. "No one can take his place."

## 10. Welcome Home

Franklin and his grandsons stood on deck as their ship sailed up the river toward Philadelphia.

Temple was twenty-five now, and Benny was a young man. But both were as excited as children. Franklin too was overjoyed at seeing America after so long.

"You know, boys," Franklin said, "I rowed down this river when I first came to Philadelphia. I was seventeen years old then. And I didn't know anyone in Philadelphia."

Just then the ship came in sight of the city. Cannons started booming and church bells ringing.

"Look at the crowds standing on the riverbank!" Benny cried. "Why, they are waving and cheering!"

A passenger near them said, "Those people are there to welcome you home, Dr. Franklin."

"Times have changed, grandfather," Benny said proudly. "Everyone in Philadelphia knows you now!"

Franklin was pleased by his welcome. He had worked hard for his country. "Now," he thought, "I have earned a rest."

But there was still work for Franklin to do. The new nation was being governed under a set of laws called the Articles of Confederation. The Articles were not strong enough to keep the states from quarreling among themselves. And Congress under the Articles was too weak to raise money, or to enforce the laws it had passed.

Many of the country's leaders felt that the Articles should be changed, and they called a "Grand Convention" for this purpose. Franklin was chosen as a delegate to the meeting.

Though Franklin was old and very tired, he went

Benjamin Franklin—president of Pennsylvania, ambassador to England and France, and spokesman for freedom. This portrait by Charles Willson Peale was painted ten months before Franklin's death.

to the meetings. The leaders talked about the Articles and finally decided to write a new set of laws—a constitution. They worked all through the summer of 1787 writing the document which we know today as the Constitution of the United States of America.

It was hard for the delegates to agree on what was best for the people. When they were all finished, many of them were not entirely happy with the document.

"No constitution can be perfect," Franklin told the men wisely. He signed the Constitution, and he urged the other delegates to sign it too.

Now Franklin could rest at last. He read books. He wrote letters to scientists. His friends and many grandchildren came to visit. Franklin was happy to see his favorite grandson, Benny, start a printing shop of his own.

Finally, in 1790, Benjamin Franklin died at the age of eighty-four.

Franklin's name will live as long as the United States lives. Cities, counties, banks, a college, and a great museum have all been named after the candlemaker's son from Boston. You can see his picture on stamps and money. His face is still almost as "well known as that of the moon."

But Benjamin Franklin is best remembered for his ideas. His ideas helped make the United States a great nation.

# The General and Dr. Franklin

## by Elizabeth Rider Montgomery

Philadelphia was usually quiet on Sundays in 1787, except for the morning clamor of church bells. Families walked to church and strolled slowly home again for a quiet dinner. All shops were closed. The streets were empty of carriages and horses.

However, the Sunday afternoon of May 13 was different. Crowds of people lined Philadelphia's main street. Shouts and cheers filled the spring air. Children laughed and clapped. The bells of Christ Church rang out, although it was long past church time. Drums rolled and fifes squealed. Carriage wheels creaked and groaned. Horses' hooves clattered on the cobblestones. The boots of blue-coated soldiers thumped out a steady marching rhythm.

The general was coming! General George Washington was coming! All of Philadelphia turned out to welcome the man who had led the American armies to victory in the War of Independence. He had come to Philadelphia as a delegate to the Grand Convention, a meeting of the new nation's leaders. In later years this meeting would be known to Americans as the Constitutional Convention.

Washington's carriage came to a halt at the corner of Fifth and High Streets. He intended to stay at a boardinghouse there.

A great crowd waited. Tall and strong, calm and dignified, George Washington climbed down a bit stiffly from his carriage. It had been a long, tiring trip. With a wave of his big hand he acknowledged the cheers of the people.

Robert Morris pushed through the crowd to greet him. Plump and red-faced, this wealthy Philadelphia merchant looked very elegant in his plum-colored suit.

"You will lodge at no boardinghouse, my friend," Morris told Washington. "Mrs. Morris and I insist that you shall be our guest during your stay in Philadelphia."

Washington smiled at his old friend. Morris took the general's arm in a firm grip. He led him to his home at 190 High Street, where Mrs. Morris greeted Washington cordially.

General Washington came to Philadelphia as one of the delegates to the Grand Convention.

While servants unpacked his clothes and hung them in the clothespress, or wardrobe, Washington brushed his suit carefully. He was getting ready to call on the man whom he considered to be the "wisest living American." That evening George Washington wrote in his diary: "As soon as I got to town, I waited on the President (of Pennsylvania), Dr. Franklin."

Benjamin Franklin, the president of Pennsylvania, sat in his favorite armchair in his upstairs library, reading.

Franklin seated at the "armonica," a musical instrument of his own invention.

There was not another chair exactly like it in the world, for Franklin had designed it himself. Above the chair was fastened a large fan that could be moved back and forth with a foot pedal. As he read, Franklin could fan himself and keep off flies at the same time, merely by moving his foot a trifle.

Although Franklin had spent much time abroad as a representative of his country, Philadelphia had been his home for more than 60 years. Now past 80, in almost constant pain, Franklin did not look at all like "the wisest living American." He was a plain-looking, stout old man, dressed in a brown suit.

Franklin "wore his own hair." That is, he did not wear a wig, and he did not powder his hair. The thin, straight gray locks hung down over his large head to his neck and looked most unfashionable. But Franklin's mind was just as active as it had been in his youth, his smile as ready and warm, his sense of humor just as strong. He loved to joke. His eyes sparkled brightly behind the bifocal glasses that he had invented for both near and far vision.

His young granddaughter Deborah ran into the room.

"Grandpapa!" she cried. "General Washington is here!"

Franklin hugged the child fondly. "Ask the general to be good enough to come upstairs," he said.

When George Washington was shown into the library, Franklin took up his walking stick and tried to rise, but Washington would not let him. He knew how painful it was for the old man to stand.

These two great Americans had not met since the early days of the war. Now the meeting between them was warm. Each had great respect for the other. Both had worked hard to help their country win its independence from England. Washington had led the soldiers on the battlefield. Franklin had made friends in France, where he obtained help for the new United States of America.

Washington looked around Franklin's big library. The walls were entirely filled with books from the floor to the high ceiling. Franklin had thousands of books—the biggest private library in America.

The old man showed his friend many of his inventions, which he called "contrivances." Washington had already seen the Franklin stove, which was like a movable fireplace. It warmed a room better than a regular fireplace and burned far less wood. This stove is still in common use today.

Washington also knew about two other popular inventions of Franklin's, the lightning rod and the "armonica," or musical glasses. But he had not seen Franklin's new invention, a rolling press for making copies of letters. Undoubtedly the general wished he had one. He had learned long ago that it was wise to keep copies of the letters he sent. A press like this would save a great deal of time.

Benjamin Franklin demonstrated the use of his "artificial arm," with which he could take books down from the highest shelf. He also showed his friend a chair that became a stepladder when the seat was lifted. Both of these Franklin "contrivances" are in common use today, especially in libraries.

Dr. Franklin surely showed Washington his electrical apparatus and other scientific machines. Both men belonged to the American Philosophical Society whose members exchanged information on science. Franklin had founded the society years before as the Junto.

Washington may have seen the old man's clever "contrivance" for bolting his bedroom door without getting out of bed, and his method of reviving a dying fire without bending over the fireplace. Later that summer Washington wrote in his diary that he had seen an ironing machine at Franklin's home, which the inventor called a "mangle." Without doubt, Benjamin Franklin was one of the most inventive men in America!

George Washington must have examined Franklin's house and his "contrivances" with deep interest. He was always looking for ways to make his beloved Mount Vernon more comfortable and more beautiful.

# Dr. Franklin's "Contrivances"

The anchor chains of these two ships could break apart in stormy seas. Franklin invented a new anchor to prevent this trouble.

Ben invented this "square of squares" as a mathematical game. Notice that the sums of each row—vertical, horizontal, and diagonal—are equal.

PLATE IV.  *A Magic Square of Squares.*  Page 360.

| 200 | 217 | 232 | 249 | 8 | 25 | 40 | 57 | 72 | 89 | 104 | 121 | 136 | 153 | 168 | 181 |
| 58 | 39 | 26 | 7 | 250 | 231 | 218 | 199 | 186 | 167 | 154 | 135 | 122 | 103 | 90 | 71 |
| 198 | 219 | 230 | 251 | 6 | 27 | 38 | 59 | 70 | 91 | 102 | 123 | 134 | 155 | 166 | 187 |
| 60 | 37 | 28 | 5 | 252 | 229 | 220 | 197 | 188 | 165 | 156 | 133 | 124 | 101 | 92 | 69 |
| 201 | 216 | 233 | 248 | 9 | 24 | 41 | 56 | 73 | 88 | 105 | 120 | 137 | 152 | 169 | 184 |
| 55 | 42 | 23 | 10 | 247 | 234 | 215 | 202 | 183 | 170 | 151 | 138 | 119 | 106 | 87 | 74 |
| 203 | 214 | 235 | 246 | 11 | 22 | 43 | 54 | 75 | 86 | 107 | 118 | 139 | 150 | 171 | 182 |
| 53 | 44 | 21 | 12 | 245 | 236 | 213 | 204 | 181 | 172 | 149 | 140 | 117 | 108 | 85 | 76 |
| 205 | 212 | 237 | 244 | 13 | 20 | 45 | 52 | 77 | 84 | 109 | 116 | 141 | 148 | 173 | 180 |
| 51 | 46 | 19 | 14 | 243 | 238 | 211 | 206 | 179 | 174 | 147 | 142 | 115 | 110 | 83 | 78 |
| 207 | 210 | 239 | 242 | 15 | 18 | 47 | 50 | 79 | 82 | 111 | 114 | 143 | 146 | 175 | 178 |
| 49 | 48 | 17 | 16 | 241 | 240 | 209 | 208 | 177 | 176 | 145 | 144 | 113 | 112 | 81 | 80 |
| 196 | 221 | 228 | 253 | 4 | 29 | 36 | 61 | 68 | 93 | 100 | 125 | 132 | 157 | 164 | 189 |
| 62 | 35 | 30 | 3 | 254 | 227 | 222 | 195 | 190 | 163 | 158 | 131 | 126 | 99 | 94 | 67 |
| 194 | 223 | 226 | 255 | 2 | 31 | 34 | 63 | 66 | 95 | 98 | 127 | 130 | 159 | 162 | 191 |
| 64 | 33 | 32 | 1 | 256 | 225 | 224 | 193 | 192 | 161 | 160 | 129 | 128 | 97 | 96 | 65 |

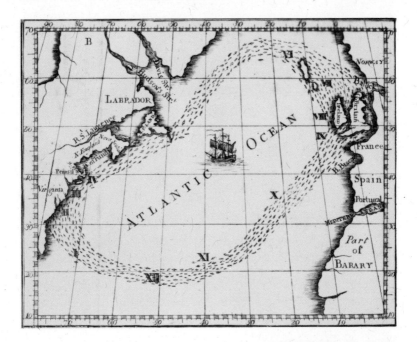

Ben plotted the Gulf Stream as an aid to sailors making the trip from Newfoundland to New York.

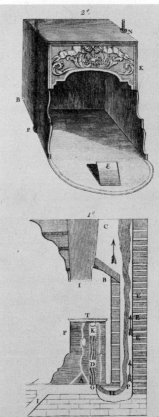

The Franklin stove not only warmed cold and drafty colonial homes, but it is still in use today.

Franklin was glad to have other people copy his ideas. He would never patent any of his inventions.

However, the two old friends surely spent most of this visit talking about the meeting that had brought George Washington to Philadelphia, the Grand Convention.

When the American Revolution ended, the thirteen United States were independent at last. But they were not really united. Each state considered itself a nation. They were jealous of each other, and they quarreled among themselves. Virginia and Pennsylvania quarreled over boundaries. New York and Connecticut threatened war against each other over a tax on firewood and farm produce.

There was no strong central government. The Continental Congress could not levy taxes. It could print paper money, but its money was nearly worthless. It could make laws, but it did not have the power to carry them out.

Nobody knew better than George Washington how helpless the Continental Congress was. During the war he had written hundreds of letters to the Congress asking for arms, shoes, and food for his starving soldiers, but Congress had sent him very little. Washington doubted that he could have won the war if Robert Morris had not supplied his army with ammunition and other necessities.

Men like Washington, Franklin, Madison, and Hamilton knew that the thirteen weak, separate states could not survive. In order to become a strong nation, the states must band together and work hard for the independence of the new nation.

So these leaders had called the Grand Convention to draw up a plan that would strengthen the central government. Delegates had been elected in each state, except Rhode Island, to attend the convention. It was to begin the next day.

"It will be a pleasure to work with you in this convention," Washington told Benjamin Franklin, and Franklin returned the general's compliment.

# George Washington

## Father of Freedom

### by Stewart Graff

## 1. Storm

Thunder rolled over the green Virginia hills. Lightning flashed against the black clouds. It was a spring afternoon in the year 1744.

Young George Washington sat easily on the big gray horse. He watched the dark clouds coming nearer. His horse began to move restlessly. George patted the big animal's neck. "Quiet, Gray," he said. Gray had been his father's horse. George was proud to ride him.

Suddenly George remembered another spring, Eastertime a year ago. He had been away from home visiting cousins. A horseman riding fast across the fields had brought the news that George's father was very sick. George had hurried home. Within a few days his father was dead. George still missed him. He often remembered the rides he and his father had taken together over the broad, rolling Virginia hills.

There was another clap of thunder. The big gray horse shied. George's legs tightened around the frightened animal.

"Race the storm, Gray," he cried, and they were

off at full gallop. But the rain came pelting down long before they reached the shelter of the barn. As George swung down from the saddle he saw another wet horse.

"Lawrence is here," he shouted. In a moment his long legs were flying as he ran to find his older brother.

Lawrence was standing in the dining room. His younger brothers and sisters were crowding around, but Lawrence was especially interested in George.

"You have grown another inch," he said. "You are almost big enough to be a planter." Lawrence turned to George's mother. "Can George come home with me for a visit?" he asked.

"I can be ready in five minutes," George answered.

His mother laughed. "Tomorrow will be time enough," she said. "You both have to dry out."

It was a long ride the next day. Lawrence and his wife, Nancy, lived in a big house called Mount Vernon. It looked down over the wide Potomac River. George liked the lively, friendly life there. Lawrence was fourteen years older than he was and seemed almost like another father.

George and Lawrence rode together every day. Once they stopped at the top of a high hill. Lawrence pointed far ahead. "Away to the west are miles and miles of forest," he said. "Someday it will be farms and towns."

## 2. The Young Soldier

During the next few years, George often visited Lawrence. Lawrence was a planter. He was also a soldier. He taught the young soldiers of Virginia how to drill and fight. Like the other American colonies, Virginia was ruled by England. But she had her own militia.

"Someday I want to be a soldier," George told Lawrence.

Lawrence smiled. "Let's think about school right now," he said.

George was sent to school in Fredericksburg, near his mother's farm. He worked hard at his studies. He was also learning many things on his visits to Mount Vernon.

Lawrence taught George how to grow tall corn and wheat and tobacco. George learned how to saddle a wild young horse. He learned how to camp and how to hunt in the woods.

When George finished school, he said to Lawrence, "I want to be a surveyor."

"I think that would be good work for you," Lawrence said. "I know surveyors in Fredericksburg who can teach you."

George worked hard. He learned to measure small plots of land for town houses. He learned to measure

George learned to be a surveyor at the age of fifteen. This engraving shows him "in the field."

and map hundreds of acres in the wilderness. Land-owners liked his work.

George still went to Mount Vernon often. Colonel Fairfax lived nearby. Pretty Sally Fairfax helped teach George to dance. Sally put her small slipper next to George's big foot. "Now step," she said. "Step!" The family laughed as tall young George struggled to learn. George laughed too.

Mount Vernon had always been a happy place for George. But it became a place of sadness too. When George was 20, Lawrence died. George knew he could take care of himself, but he missed his older brother.

George became a successful surveyor. After Lawrence died, Mount Vernon became George's home.

George liked having his own land. "But someone must take my brother Lawrence's place training the soldiers," George said. "I believe I can do it." So he went to see the governor.

Governor Dinwiddie liked the calm steadiness in George's eyes. He felt a quiet power in the younger man.

"You are only 20," the governor said, "but I will give you the chance."

George became Major George Washington of the Virginia militia.

## 3. A Dangerous Ride

One day Governor Dinwiddie sent for George. "I have bad news," he said. "Indian traders say the French are building forts in the Ohio River valley."

The rich Ohio country was across the mountains to the west. Both England and France claimed it.

"England must control the Ohio valley," Governor Dinwiddie said to George. "It is rich land. Take this letter to the French commander. It tells him he must leave."

On a cold November day George set out on the long ride. There were seven men in his party. One of them was Christopher Gist, a woodsman and guide. The men rode over the rough mountain trails to the Ohio country.

"We had rains, snows and bad traveling through many miles," George wrote. Two friendly Indian chiefs named Half King and White Thunder helped them find the way.

At last they reached the French fort. George gave his letter to the French commander. The commander was polite to George, but his answer was firm.

"This country belongs to France," the commander said. "No Englishman can even trade here."

George told Christopher, "We must warn the governor. The French will build new forts in the spring."

The trip back was hard and slow. The weather grew worse. "Our horses were weak and feeble. They grew less able to travel every day," George wrote later. George knew he must hurry. "I decided to take the nearest way through the woods on foot."

George and Christopher left the others to follow. They hurried on alone. It was hard walking. The snow was deep.

There were other troubles. "In a place called the Murdering Town, Indians had lain in wait for us," George wrote. "One of them fired, but fortunately missed. We walked all the rest of the night to be out of reach."

This old print shows George Washington and his friend, Christopher Gist, crossing the Allegheny.

Finally they came to the broad Allegheny River. Big flat cakes of ice bobbed in the black, swift water.

"We must make a raft," Christopher said. "It is the only way we will be able to cross."

They worked all day to build the raft. The sun had just set when they finished. They poled the raft into the black water. The swift current carried them downstream. Suddenly the raft lurched. George slipped.

"Look out!" shouted Christopher.

It was too late. George was thrown into the icy water. He caught the raft just in time. It took all his strength to pull himself back on. The raft swept on toward land, a little island in the river.

They could not go on. The long, cold night closed in. The first gray daylight brought a welcome sight. The river had frozen over, and the ice was thick enough to hold them. They walked to the other shore.

Ten miles further on they came to a lonely trader's house. There they found a warm fire and hot food. George borrowed horses.

"We must ride fast," George told Christopher. "We must tell the governor that the French mean war."

## 4. Indian Fighters

Governor Dinwiddie talked to George about the French plans. "I am sending you back to the Ohio country," Governor Dinwiddie told George. "This time you will take soldiers. We will build a fort at the head of the Ohio River."

George and his men marched toward the river. Indians brought bad news. The French had already built a fort there. Now France controlled the Ohio country.

George knew he could not defeat the French. They were too strong. Indians were helping them. George built a little fort and called it Fort Necessity.

Early one morning the crack of French rifles cut the air. The battle lasted all day. George did not have enough men. Finally he had to surrender.

"Your soldiers can go free," the French commander told George. "But they must leave the Ohio country." Washington and his men began the slow march back to Virginia.

People welcomed George home. They knew he had fought bravely.

Soon George heard that more soldiers had arrived from England. They would help fight the French. An Englishman, General Braddock, was their commander. George helped guide Braddock's army west over the mountains. The soldiers were nearing the French fort when the French and Indians struck. They opened fire from the tall grass and from behind trees and rocks. Indian war cries rang through the air. The

George as an officer in the Virginia militia, and
Martha Custis as a young widow.

English soldiers fired back, but they could not see
the enemy.

A French bullet ripped George's hat. Two more
bullets cut through his uniform. Two of his horses
were shot and killed. The English soldiers lost the
battle. Sadly, the army retreated to Virginia.

George was unhappy about losing the battle. But,
for a special reason, he was glad to be home. He
often called on a pretty young widow. Her name was
Martha Custis. Martha would smile up at the tall,
young colonel when they danced. "I think you are
happier on a horse than on the dance floor," Martha
teased him.

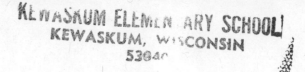
The war with France was not over. Once more the English and the men from Virginia marched against the French fort. This time General Forbes was their commander. He asked George to lead the Virginia soldiers.

The march ended in victory for the English. The French burned their fort and fled. England had control of the Ohio country at last.

George had missed Martha during the long and dangerous march. He began to realize how much she meant to him.

As soon as the English had won, George hurried back home. Martha Custis was waiting.

## 5. Mount Vernon

The day was January 6, 1759. Cheerful fires burned in the Custis house. There was a hum of voices and laughter. Then there was quiet as the minister married George and Martha. Young Colonel Washington smiled down happily at his bride.

A busy new life began for George. He had been away from Mount Vernon too long. "Every barn and fence and shed needs repairing," he told Martha.

George was happy with his new family. Martha's first husband had died leaving her with two children. Jackie was four years old, and a little girl, Patsy, was two years younger. Jackie and Patsy made Mount Vernon a lively place.

Soon Jackie was old enough to ride with his step-father. "He will be a good horseman," George told Martha. "I can teach him to ride with me in the fox hunts. He will like that."

Patsy liked music. George gave her a new piano. "As for myself I do not know one note from another," George said. But in the evening he liked to sit in the candlelight and hear Patsy play.

The happy days at Mount Vernon lasted fifteen years. George made Mount Vernon a large, successful plantation. He became one of the most important men of Virginia.

He was elected to the Virginia House of Burgesses. The Burgesses made most of the laws for the colony. England made the others. George learned what laws worked best. He learned how to plan new laws.

Trouble was beginning for Virginia and the other colonies. England made laws the colonists believed would take away their freedom. The colonists hated the English taxes most of all.

"It is unfair for England to make us pay taxes," George said to Martha. "We do not have men to represent us in the English government."

The angry colonists sent men to a meeting in Philadelphia. "We will try to make England change the laws," they said. The meeting was called the Continental Congress. George was one of the men chosen to represent the colony of Virginia.

England would not listen to the colonies. "There may be war," George told Martha. "Many Americans say we must fight for our rights."

The quarrel with England became worse. Sharp fighting broke out in Massachusetts. English soldiers took over Boston. American soldiers camped outside the city. They were brave fighters, but they were not an army. They needed to learn to march and work and

The British retreated from Lexington and Concord under attack by American villagers and farmers. It was the first battle of the American Revolution.

fight together. They needed officers, and they needed a general.

Congress knew Washington was a good soldier and a strong leader. Congress named George Washington as general of the first American army.

George was sad to leave his family. He wrote to Martha, "My dearest. I would find more happiness in one month with you in Mount Vernon than in 50 years at war. But the American cause is being put under my care."

## 6. The Trap

Washington worked hard to train the army. He appointed officers. He tried to get enough food and guns.

It took months to get the big guns the army needed. Washington wanted to attack the British in Boston. "Put the cannons on the highest hills," he ordered.

The men worked silently under a cold winter moon. At dawn the British saw the cannons. They knew American gunners could blast the city. The British did not have enough men to risk an attack. They sailed away from Boston.

"The British will go on fighting," Washington told his men. "We must be ready to meet their next attack. I believe it will be at New York." Washington marched his men south over the dusty roads.

Washington had guessed right. Early one morning in New York, an excited messenger came running. "British ships are coming, sir, one after the other!" he exclaimed.

By night almost 100 English ships were sighted off New York. For days the enemy ships kept coming. They were carrying more than 30,000 soldiers.

"Our army is much smaller than the British army," Washington told his men, "but we must defend New York."

Important news came from the Continental Congress in Philadelphia. Congress had passed the Declaration of Independence on July 4, 1776. The Declaration said the American colonies were free from England.

"Read the Declaration to all the soldiers," Washington ordered. "Now they will know their country depends on them." The soldiers roared out their cheers. They had been fighting for their rights. Now they were fighting for something even more important—their independence.

The English attacked on Long Island across the wide East River. The battle lines formed. Washington stayed with his men. The fight began. Bullets whined through the trees and bushes. Shouts rang out above the crack of rifle fire. Bayonets flashed. Rifle butts swung like clubs. American and British blood soaked the ground. Quiet bodies lay where men had fallen.

The American army fought bravely, but it was beaten. The army retreated to the forts Washington had built in the hills above the East River. New York was across the river.

"We must act quickly or we will be trapped," Washington said. "The English warships will sail up the river and block us from New York."

Washington sent for every small boat within miles. That night he ordered his men to the shore.

Through the dark night sweating men rowed the little boats back and forth to New York. All through the night Washington stood by the river. Sometimes he gave an order. Always the men saw his tall figure.

Morning came. Fog covered the hills and the river. Not a sound came from the American forts.

"Send out scouts," ordered the English commander. Soon the scouts ran back with the news. Every American was gone! Washington's army had broken out of the trap.

Washington had saved his army, but he was not strong enough to defeat the British. The British drove the Americans out of New York. They drove them from the rocky hills beyond the city. They followed them across New Jersey. Washington and his army retreated across the Delaware River into Pennsylvania.

## 7. Victory or Death

The cold, dark days of early winter began. The British general thought the fighting was over for the winter. He sent many of his soldiers back across New Jersey to New York City.

Washington's soldiers were weak and ragged. Americans were discouraged. It seemed they could never win now. But Washington gave them a new password: "Victory or Death."

It was six o'clock on Christmas evening, 1776. The Americans waited in the darkness for orders to march.

The men moved slowly across the slippery snow to the bank of the Delaware River. They climbed into small boats. Floating ice filled the dark river.

Washington crossed the river. He stood on the shore. His cloak was wrapped closely around him against the bitter cold. He gave his orders quietly. "Keep your soldiers together," he told his officers. "There is a long march ahead."

It was late night before all the soldiers were finally across the river. Washington called his officers together. "Tell the men we will attack at Trenton," Washington said. "We will surprise the enemy."

The men began the slow, cold march. Many soldiers had only rags for shoes. Their cut, bruised feet left blood on the snow.

A detail from *Washington Crossing the Delaware*, a painting by Emanuel Leutze.

By daylight the Americans were at Trenton. Hessian soldiers were there. They were hard-fighting men from Germany. Their prince had paid them to fight for the British.

The first crack of rifle shots brought the Hessians tumbling from their houses. The officers did not have time to tell their men what to do. "Fire!" they shouted. The Hessians tried to fire, but it was too late. American cannonballs and bullets were already splintering the walls of the houses and smashing through the windows. The Hessians surrendered.

Washington had captured Trenton. Americans cheered the news. "We can fight back! We can win!" they told each other.

Washington thought the Americans could win another victory. But it was time for many of the men to go home. They had promised to be soldiers only for a short time, and now they wanted to leave. Washington knew that he must keep his men fighting. "Call the men together," he ordered.

General Washington rode his horse slowly along the lines of ragged men. His tall figure towered in the saddle.

"You have done all I asked you to do and more," he said to them. "But your country, your wives, your homes, and everything you love is at stake. You have worn yourselves out, but I do not know how to spare you. Stay one month longer, and you will serve your country in a way you never can again."

The drums rolled. Then there was silence. One by one, the soldiers stepped forward. They would stay. Washington had saved his army for another battle.

## 8. Valley Forge

Washington attacked next at the little town of Princeton. The fight was short and savage. Washington was in the thick of the battle. A young officer who was near him wrote home to his wife, "I shall never forget what I felt when I saw Washington brave all the dangers with a thousand deaths flying around him."

The British line broke and their soldiers ran. Washington shouted to his men, "It is a fine fox chase, my boys!" The Americans raced to take prisoners.

Washington's men had stayed with him for the battle. But now many of them went home. The colonies would send new soldiers in the spring. Washington tried to hold together what was left of his small army. Sometimes he felt as if there were no hope.

"How we shall be able to rub along till the new army is raised, I know not," he wrote.

Washington was sure the English would attack when good weather began. He must be patient and wait.

Finally the British moved against Philadelphia. Once

Tattered soldiers huddled around campfires for warmth during the bitter winter at Valley Forge.

again Washington tried to keep the British from taking an important American city. Once again Washington lost. The British took Philadelphia in the autumn.

"We must camp outside Philadelphia for the winter," Washington wrote to Congress. He chose a place called Valley Forge.

The cold weather set in. Snow fell, and icy winds blew across the hills. The shivering American soldiers tried to keep warm, but there was only green wood to burn. They cut logs and built cabins. There were not enough blankets. The soldiers' clothes and shoes were worn out, and many men were in rags.

There was almost no food. The soldiers had a bitter joke. "What's for dinner, sir?" The answer was always, "Fire cake and water." Fire cake was a rough bread cooked over a campfire. Many men became weak and sick. Many died.

The long months seemed without hope. But day after day men lived on. They knew Washington was with them. Soldiers on guard in the cold, lonely night watched for his tall figure. The men waited for his word of greeting. Then somehow they felt better.

Washington did not lose hope. He worked to keep his men alive. He asked the governors of the colonies to send food and clothes and blankets. But he knew something else was needed for the army.

"Our soldiers must have better training," Washington told his officers.

The officers worked long days drilling the soldiers. "Forward! Fire! Charge!" The commands rang across the hard-packed snow on the drill field. The men learned to move quickly in answer to orders.

The warm days of spring came at last. The men had better clothes and food. Most important, they were trained soldiers.

On April 30, 1778, exciting news came. A messenger galloped into camp bringing a letter from Congress. The letter said that France would help the colonies. Washington called his officers.

"Tell the men we no longer fight alone," he said. "France will help us."

When the soldiers heard the news, cheers rang through the camp. At last there was real hope that America would win.

Washington ordered a parade. The soldiers were thin. Their clothes were patched. But they put dogwood flowers in their hats, and they marched with their heads high. Their lines were straight. Their step was quick.

George Washington watched the soldiers proudly. They had lived through the bitter, killing winter of Valley Forge. Now they were trained to fight.

## 9. By Land and by Sea

In late May a spy came into Washington's camp with good news. "The British are getting ready to leave Philadelphia," he said.

The British knew the American army was getting stronger. They also knew French ships and soldiers were on their way to help the Americans. They decided to retreat to New York. The British soldiers marched from Philadelphia, across New Jersey. Burning heat settled down.

"This is our chance to attack," Washington said.

The Americans attacked the British near the village

of Monmouth. The sharp crack of American rifles cut through the blanket of heat. The fight was on.

The battle raged all day. Now the training of Valley Forge showed. The Americans fought the big British army to a standstill. The British retreated to New York. Slowly the tide of the war was turning.

Still the British army stayed in New York. The British fleet was in the harbor.

"We dare not attack New York," Washington wrote to Congress. "We are not strong enough."

Months went by before Washington was ready to attack again. Then he went south to Virginia. The British had another big army there commanded by Lord Cornwallis.

Washington saw his chance for victory. "Our soldiers will attack by land," he told his officers. "The French are helping us. Their fleet will close in from the sea."

The Americans and the French trapped Cornwallis at Yorktown. The roar of the cannon began. Shell after shell ripped into the British lines. There was no way for the British army to escape. On October 19, 1781, the British surrendered.

Washington ordered his soldiers to stand along the road from Yorktown. It was a warm sunny day. Washington rode to the head of the line. His thoughts went back over the six long years of war. He remembered the hard marches and the bitter defeats.

As the last British troops left New York, General Washington said good-bye to his officers at Fraunces Tavern. Painting by Alonzo Chappel.

He remembered the soldiers who had died. Now a powerful British army was surrendering. It was a great victory for America.

Drums beat in the distance. The British were marching out of Yorktown. Washington heard the first sounds from the British band. For a moment he smiled. The band was playing "The World Turned Upside Down."

Washington watched the British soldiers lay down their rifles on the ground as they left.

The war dragged on for two more years, but the real fighting was over. Peace came at last. The thirteen colonies were free. They were now the United States of America.

The last English soldiers left New York in November of 1783. Now General Washington could go back home to Virginia.

On December 4, Washington said good-bye to his officers at Fraunces Tavern in New York. The eight long years of work and struggle were over. Washington looked at his officers and said, "With a heart full of love and gratitude I now take leave of you."

One by one Washington's officers came to him and shook his hand. At the last they had no words to say. There were tears in their eyes. There were tears in Washington's eyes too.

## 10. The First President

On the first day at home Washington was up early. His favorite horse, Nelson, was saddled and waiting for him. Washington rode fast over Mount Vernon's frozen fields. It was dinnertime before he came back.

"All the years I was away I made plans for making Mount Vernon better," Washington told Martha. "Now we can begin."

Life at Mount Vernon was busy, but Washington did not forget his country. He worried about the new government. He knew it did not have enough power to rule the country.

Finally the new states sent delegates to Philadelphia to plan a better government. Washington was one of the men from Virginia.

Each delegate at the meeting had his own plans about what to do. "We need someone to lead the meeting," Benjamin Franklin said. "Otherwise we will be crowing out our ideas like a barnyard of roosters." The men elected Washington to be their leader.

In later years this meeting in Philadelphia would be known as the Constitutional Convention. The delegates planned a new and stronger government. They wrote down the powers it should have. They called their new plan of government the Constitution of the United States.

General Washington was happy to become a farmer once more at his beloved Mount Vernon.

The Constitution said there should be a Congress to make laws, and courts to settle arguments about what laws mean. The Constitution also said there should be a president to head the government. He was to carry out the laws Congress made. The people knew the one man they trusted most. They elected George Washington as their first president.

Washington was sad to leave Mount Vernon, but the country needed him. He became the first president on April 30, 1789.

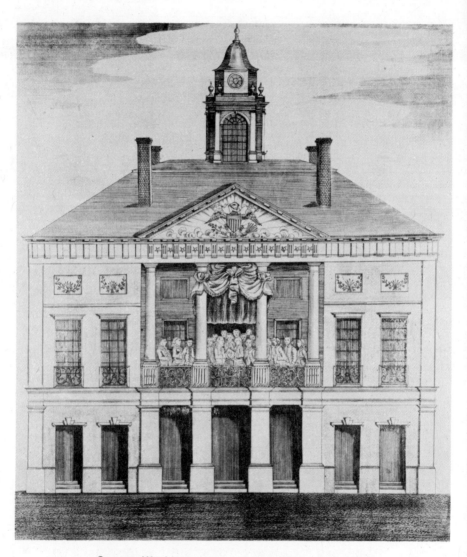

George Washington was inaugurated as the first
president of the United States on the balcony of
Federal Hall in New York City.

The capital of the United States was then New York. There was a parade down the city streets. The harbor was crowded with ships flying their flags. A 21-gun salute was fired. Soldiers marched. People cheered when they saw Washington's big yellow coach drawn by cream-colored horses.

There had never been a president before. "How will he act?" the people asked.

Some were afraid the president would turn into a king. "Fine folk would spoil our General, if they could," one old soldier wrote. "He never was a greater man than when he rode among us with his dusty boots."

But people soon stopped worrying, for Washington did not act like a king. He did not try to run the country alone. He asked other leaders for their ideas, and he chose the best people in the country to help him. He traveled throughout the country to find out what people were thinking.

There had never been a government like this one. Washington knew everything the government did was important for the future. He planned his actions carefully. He had to make the new government work.

America began to grow. Factories hummed in the new nation. Farm crops filled the big barns. George Washington had led his country in war. Now he led it in peace.

## 11. "First in War, First in Peace"

Washington served four years as president. Then the people reelected him. The capital was now in Philadelphia.

Washington found the United States had many new problems. People did not always agree on how to deal with these problems. They began to join with others who held the same beliefs to form political parties.

Alexander Hamilton and Thomas Jefferson, two of the president's closest advisers, were the leaders of the two political parties. Each man argued for his own ideas. Soon they became bitter enemies. Washington was saddened by the break between his two aides.

Before long Washington had to face another problem. The new government needed money. Congress passed tax laws. One law made people pay a tax for making whiskey. Men in western Pennsylvania were angry.

"Down with the tax!" they cried. "We will fight before we pay it!" The men got out their guns.

"This tax is an important test," Washington said. "The laws of the United States must be obeyed."

Washington called out United States soldiers. Once again men in uniform made the long march over the mountains to western Pennsylvania. The revolt ended without a battle.

President George Washington. His actions as the nation's first chief executive would influence the American presidency for generations to come.

Washington also had to deal with troubles abroad. France and England were at war. Many Americans wanted to help France. They remembered how France had helped their young nation win her freedom.

President Washington spoke for the country. "We fought for our independence," he said. "We must stay independent. We are not strong enough yet to help other countries."

Many people were angry, but George Washington stood firm.

The troubles with England grew worse. England would not honor part of the treaty that ended the Revolutionary War. She refused to give up forts at Detroit and in the country along the Great Lakes north of the Ohio River valley. At the forts English traders were selling guns and supplies to the Indians who were keeping American settlers from the rich Ohio lands.

The war between England and France dragged on. The English navy was seizing American ships trading with France and France's colonies in the West Indies. Captured American sailors were forced to join the English navy. The call for war with England was rumbling across the country like thunder.

Washington sent John Jay, the chief justice of the United States Supreme Court, to England to try to find a way to peace. Jay made the best treaty he could. England gave up the forts, but many Americans believed the treaty was unfair to the United States in other ways. They said America should fight England, and they blamed Washington and Jay for the treaty.

"We cannot listen to the angry voices," Washington said. "The treaty will keep us at peace. We must have peace in order to grow strong."

Most people trusted Washington to know what to do. Congress accepted the treaty.

There was trouble with Spain too. Spain held the port of New Orleans at the mouth of the Mississippi River. Spain would not let ships from the United States use the river to trade with other countries.

Washington sent Thomas Pinckney to settle the troubles with Spain. He waited anxiously for news.

Washington's birthday, February 22, 1796, gave him a chance to forget his worries. The country celebrated the president's birthday. Church bells rang. Cannons were fired. Crowds flocked to the president's house.

During the day the news arrived that a treaty with Spain was signed. "This is the best birthday present of all," Washington told Martha. "Spain says that Americans may now use all of the Mississippi River. People in the West will cheer this news."

Washington was also busy planning a new capital city for the United States. Later the city was named Washington for the president.

*The Washington Family* by Edward Savage

President Washington finished his second term. Many people wanted him to be president again. "No," he said, "I believe it is time for another man." Washington's work was done.

On the move back to Mount Vernon, wagons carried the furniture. Martha insisted that the parrot and their pet dog, Vulcan, ride in the carriage with them. The parrot screamed. Vulcan barked. "It sounds like a battlefield," George said with a smile.

Washington went home to Mount Vernon and the life he and Martha loved. In the long days of spring Washington was up with the sun. He watched the work being done on Mount Vernon's buildings.

"There is the music of hammers and the smell of paint everywhere," he wrote to a friend.

Washington rode over the farms of Mount Vernon. He planned the crops. He watched the wheat fields ripen and the young colts racing in the pastures.

Martha's grandchildren, George and Nelly Custis, were growing up. Their laughter brightened the house.

On Washington's birthday in 1799, there was a happy wedding at Mount Vernon. Nelly Custis was married to Washington's nephew, Lawrence Lewis. Guests filled the bright rooms. Washington watched the festivities proudly.

The year neared its end. One cold day in December 1799, Washington went riding through the fields. A winter storm broke. Washington was wet and cold when he reached home. His hair was caked with ice.

That evening he felt sick. During the night he could hardly breathe. Martha knew he was desperately ill. The doctors came. They did their best, but by the next evening George Washington was dead.

Americans mourned. Washington had led them to victory and freedom. He had been their first president. "He was the father of our country," people said.

One of Washington's old soldiers remembered him with these great words that have lived across the years: "first in war, first in peace, and first in the hearts of his countrymen."

# A Walk in Freedom's City

*by Elizabeth Rider Montgomery*

From *Old Ben Franklin's Philadelphia* by Elizabeth Rider Montgomery (Champaign, Illinois: 1967). Reprinted by permission of the author.

The morning after George Washington's arrival in Philadelphia, he rose early as usual. When breakfast was over, he set out for the State House where the Grand Convention would be held.

It was only two blocks from the Morris home to the State House. However, Washington liked to walk around the city, so he probably went several blocks out of his way.

Philadelphia was a busy, noisy city. Carriages clattered on the cobblestones, taking wealthy businessmen like Robert Morris to their offices. Heavy wagons rumbled toward the docks, where sailing ships waited for their cargoes. Horses neighed. Drivers shouted. Pigs squealed and ran from screeching wheels. Children shouted and laughed on their way to school.

The din was terrific. People who wanted to talk had to step inside a tavern or a shop in order to hear each other's words.

"What terrible traffic!" people complained. "Did you ever in your life see so many horses and carriages?"

Then somebody was sure to reply, "One thing is certain: Traffic is as bad as it can possibly get."

Philadelphia streets were the same level as the brick sidewalks, called "pavements." There were no curbs. Strong cedar posts were placed along the edge of the sidewalks to keep horses off so pedestrians would not be hurt.

The sidewalks swarmed with people. Carpenters, bricklayers, and painters hurried along, carrying the tools of their trades. Apprenticed boys pushed wheelbarrows, piled high with paper for a printshop, or bright cloth for a tailor shop, or beaver skins for a hat shop.

In summer the unpaved streets were inches deep in dust. Washington was glad for the long spell of rainy weather that had kept the dust down. But the mud that replaced the dust, especially through the winter, was even worse. Then the streets would be so mucky that a gentleman would mount his horse merely to cross the street, to avoid wading in the mud. A lady was usually carried from her coach to her front door.

Philadelphia, halfway between Maine and Georgia,

The corner of Third and Market Streets in the heart of Philadelphia's thriving business section.

was now the greatest city in America. More than 40,000 people lived there. "No other city could boast of so many streets, so many houses, so many people, so much renown," one traveler wrote. "No other city was so rich, so extravagant, so fashionable."

Yet, all kinds of trash and garbage were thrown into the streets. There wasn't any sewage or garbage disposal then. Pigs were allowed to run in the streets, and they ate the refuse. The smells of garbage, sewage, and horse manure mingled to make a mighty stench.

The streets were not only noisy and smelly, but were bright with color too. The dazzling spring sunshine glinted on gaily painted awnings and balconies. It shone on hundreds of colored signs.

There were no street markers in Philadelphia at that time, and no numbers on the doors of shops or houses. When a stranger asked directions, he was not told to look for a certain street, but to look for a certain sign.

Standing on the corner of a business street, George Washington would have seen dozens of brightly colored picture-signs swinging in the breeze. Many people could not read or write, so merchants used pictures instead of their names in front of their shops. Washington might have seen pictures of hats, wigs, shoes, dresses, books, barrels, clocks, candles, guns, wheels, anchors, bread, and so on.

In addition, he would have seen the brilliant signs that illustrated the names of the taverns, such as "The Indian Queen," "A Plume of Feathers," "The Pewter Platter," "The Lion," "The White Horse," "The Black Horse," "The Three Crowns," "The Lemon Tree," "Noah's Ark," "The Star and Garter."

All of these picture-signs were painted in bright colors on wood, and they hung in front of the inns. Some of them had been painted by Philadelphia's finest artists.

The Franklin Inn had an excellent portrait of Benjamin Franklin, with this verse underneath:

Come view your patriot Father!
    And your Friend,
And toast to Freedom and to
    slavery's end.

Another tavern displayed this verse:

I, William McDermott, lives here;
I sells good porter, ale, and beer;
I've made my sign a little wider
To let you know I sell good cider.

No doubt many of the passersby pushing and jostling their way through the crowds that morning noticed the straight, soldierly general striding along the street. After the peaceful months at Mount Vernon, he delighted in the busy life of the city.

If Washington had walked past the riverfront, he could have seen as many as 100 ships tied up at the long wharves, or sailing up or down the river. Some of them probably belonged to his host, Robert Morris.

Philadelphia was more than 100 miles from the ocean. This was too far for any salt air or sea breeze to reach the city, but in every other way Philadelphia

*Mariner.*

was an ocean port. Ships came up the Delaware River to unload goods from Europe, the West Indies, and the Orient.

Workmen in leather aprons carried boxes and bales down the gangplanks and piled them on the pavements. Other men loaded them on wagons, to be taken to Philadelphia warehouses and stores, or to other parts of Pennsylvania. Ships' officers bawled out orders at the tops of their voices. Workmen shouted and joked as they labored. Horses pawed the cobblestones restlessly as they waited for their wagons to be loaded. Anchor chains rattled, winches creaked, wheels screeched.

Big wagons brought goods to be shipped out. Here was a wagon packed carefully with fine furniture. There was one stacked high with crates of live chickens and another loaded with new lumber. Other wagons carried hats, shoes, books, and tools.

When a ship's cargo was safely stowed on board and its supplies of food and water loaded, the ship set sail if the tide was high. It would sail down the

Shipwright

Philadelphia's bustling waterfront in 1801. The great trade center was a port of call for hundreds of ocean-going ships each year.

Delaware River and out to the Atlantic Ocean. Months would pass before it would complete its voyage and return to the great inland port of Philadelphia.

Along the waterfront were many business houses and shops to serve sailors and shipowners. There were taverns, coffeehouses, warehouses, and a customshouse. There were also many shops for outfitting ships with such items as ropes, sails, riggings, and cabinets. So many ships were outfitted in the port of Philadelphia, that a common saying was, "The ship has a Boston bottom and a Philadelphia top."

Washington did not need his eyes to locate the fish markets. They could be found by the sense of smell, and there were many of them. If the main business section of Philadelphia had seemed odorous to Washington, the waterfront reeked! The smells of decaying fish, drainage ditches, and the usual street smells of horses and ancient garbage combined with the odor of old ships, new lumber, tar, and rope.

When the general passed the great clock on the dock, he realized that the hour was late. The first meeting of the Grand Convention was about to begin! Washington pulled out his pocketwatch, hastily set the time, and walked quickly off to the State House. Today, of all days, it would never do to be late!

# Thomas Jefferson

## Author of Independence

*by Anne Colver*

## 1. Indian Paddle

One bright September morning in 1753 young Thomas Jefferson was up at sunrise. He pulled on a faded cotton shirt and trousers. He crept quietly to the door. He mustn't wake his little brother Randolph, who slept in the same room. His four sisters were still sleeping across the hall.

Tom tiptoed to the stairs. He hoped his mother and father wouldn't hear him. His mother would make him go back to comb his thick, red hair. She always wanted Tom to look neat, but Tom never cared how he looked. His lively, gray eyes were too busy looking at the world. He wrote down notes about everything he saw.

"Tom was born curious," his father said. "He wants to learn everything!"

This was the last day of vacation. The sun was just peeping over the green Virginia hills. Tom ran to the stables to saddle his horse Dandy. Tom's father had let him choose the colt to train for his own.

Tom swung into the saddle and headed toward the river path. His long legs seemed at home on a horse.

The Rivanna River ran through Tom's father's fields. Tom's father was Peter Jefferson. He had been one of the first to settle in the wild country of western Virginia. Peter Jefferson had cleared his own land and helped build his house. He planted wheat and tobacco on his big plantation.

At the river's edge, the path was narrow. Tom saw his canoe on the shore. He looked across the river at a small mountain. It was his favorite place. He and his sister Jane liked to have picnics there. The oak trees at the top seemed to reach up to the blue sky. Jane understood how much Tom loved his "little mountain."

"Come on, Dandy!" Tom dug his heels, and the horse sprang to a gallop. Tom lifted his freckled face to the wind. He liked to ride fast.

When Tom came home he found a surprise. Jane was waiting for him. "Hurry," she said. "Chief Ontassette has come to visit papa. He has a present for you."

Ontassette was chief of the Cherokee Indians. Tom's father had many good friends among the Indians. The chief often visited the Jefferson family.

Tom hurried to the house. He bowed politely to the tall Indian. The chief's present was a new Indian paddle for Tom's canoe.

At supper Tom asked the chief questions: "How do

Indians make birch bark canoes? What kind of corn do they plant? What is the Indian word for water? And for horse and tree and moon and dog?"

Tom's mother interrupted him. She was always very careful about manners. "Not so many questions, Tom," she smiled. "You cannot learn everything at once."

Later, on their way to bed, Tom's father and mother stopped to look at the children. Tom was smiling in his sleep. "I never saw such a boy for *living*," his mother whispered. "He enjoys every minute of a day. Even when he goes to sleep he is already enjoying tomorrow!"

## 2. Full Moon

The Jefferson house was called Shadwell. It was on the road to Williamsburg, the capital of Virginia. Travelers often stopped to visit. Like other Virginia families, the Jeffersons welcomed company.

Tom was the oldest son. His father loved the outdoors. He taught Tom to ride and hunt and fish.

Tom's father, Peter Jefferson, was not only a planter, he was a surveyor. That meant he measured land. He had helped make the first map of Virginia. He was also a judge.

"A judge must try to understand people," Tom's

father said. "It doesn't matter who people are or where they come from. People should all be treated fairly."

Tom's father had not had the chance to go to school for long, but he had read many books and taught himself. Tom and his sister Jane loved their father's books. "But Tom must go to school," his father said. "He must have a real education."

Tom studied hard at school. He liked to know how machines worked. He liked new ideas.

One day a visitor brought a violin to Shadwell.

This early painting shows colonial gentlemen riding to the hunt as young Tom did.

Tom listened to him play. Tom asked if he could try it. He picked out a tune.

The next time Tom's father went to Williamsburg he bought Tom a violin. Jane played the clavichord, which was like a piano. She taught Tom the notes. She and Tom played together. Tom's feet kept time to his fiddle.

"You'll soon be dancing with the girls," Jane teased.

"Not with my big feet," Tom shook his head. "They would trip up any girl."

The summer Tom was fourteen his father promised they would visit the Indian camp of Chief Ontassette. "We will go in the full moon," he said.

The next week Tom's father was ill. One night, Tom was called to his father's room. Peter Jefferson said, "You must take my place now, Tom. You will be the man of the family." Tom nodded. He could not speak. The full moon shone across his father's bed.

The next day Tom's father died. He left all his property to Tom and to Tom's younger brother. Tom must manage the plantation and the sixty men who worked for his father. He must take care of his mother and sisters. It was a big job for a fourteen-year-old boy.

But·Tom had learned about the crops from his father. He knew when to plant and how to harvest. The men did not mind taking orders from their new master. Tom was young, but he was kind and fair, like his father. And he worked as hard as any of them.

## 3. Saddlebags

Tom would have gone on working on the plantation. But when fall came his mother said, "You must go on to school, Tom. Your father would not want you to stop."

Tom went away to school. It was too far to come home each day. Tom packed his saddlebags. His fiddle was under one arm. He bent to kiss his mother's cheek. "I will come home every Saturday," he promised. "Jane and Martha will help you with the younger children. You mustn't worry."

Tom was happy at school. There was a library with many books. Tom learned Greek and Latin and French. Tom's teacher saw that Tom liked to write. "You must love words to use them well," he told Tom.

Tom liked other things at school. The boys were friendly. Tom's best friend was Dabney Carr.

Tom often brought Dabney home to Shadwell. Dabney was just like another brother in the family. The boys went fishing together. They would climb Tom's little mountain and cook their supper on top. Over the fire, they told each other what they hoped to do when they became older.

Tom had one special dream. He wanted to build a house on his little mountain. One day he looked down from the mountain at the pretty town of Charlottesville and the green hills beyond.

"This is the most beautiful place in the whole world," he said.

"How do you know?" Dabney asked. "You haven't seen the whole world."

"I don't have to," Tom said. He was sure his little mountain was the best.

Another day the boys talked about dying. "I'd like to be buried under that big oak tree," Tom said.

"So would I," Dabney said. "Let's promise each other that whoever dies first, the other will bury him right there." They shook hands.

A few minutes later the boys were eating fried fish. They had forgotten all about dying. "My father settled this land," Tom said. "I guess I feel related to everything on it."

Dabney took a big mouthful of trout. "I hope you don't feel related to the fish," he said. "If you do, we are eating your cousin!"

When Tom was seventeen he entered the College of William and Mary in Williamsburg. He liked his new studies, especially science. He wrote to Jane: "Science is the study of how the world works!" He brought home many new books.

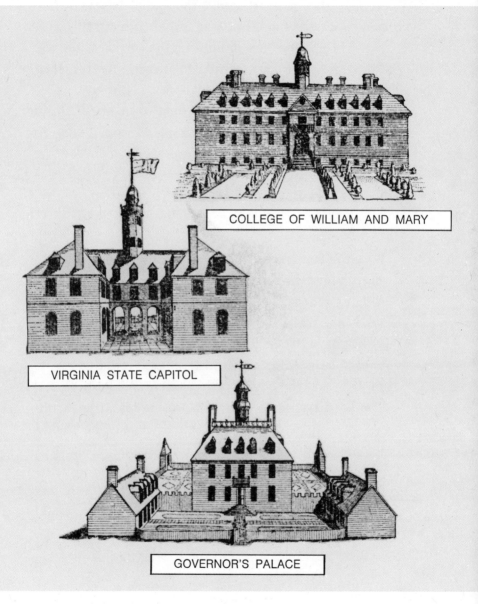

COLLEGE OF WILLIAM AND MARY

VIRGINIA STATE CAPITOL

GOVERNOR'S PALACE

At first the other students thought Tom spent too much time studying. But one evening he went to a party. He played his fiddle and danced with the prettiest girls. He had learned to manage his big feet. The boys saw that Tom liked to have fun too.

Tom did well in college. He then went on to study law. He never forgot his teachers. "I was lucky to have the best of teachers," Tom wrote many years later. "They fixed my destiny."

## 4. Monticello

In 1767 Tom passed his examinations. Now he was a lawyer, and he had an office.

Although Tom was kept busy with his new duties, he did not forget his family. He went home often. One bright summer day Dabney Carr married Tom's youngest sister Martha. It was a gay wedding. Now Tom felt that he and Dabney were really brothers.

Tom had begun to clear the top of his little mountain. As soon as he earned enough money he would build his house. "I know what I will name it," he told Dabney. "In Italian 'little mountain' is *monticello*. I will call my house Monticello."

Tom drew pictures to show how the house would look. He thought of many inventions. He drew a picture of a little elevator. It could carry hot food from the kitchen up to the dining room. He would have a bed that pulled up to the ceiling on ropes. It would be out of the way in the daytime. He put his ideas in a notebook.

It was nearly four years before Tom could start building his house. Before it was finished, Tom had bad news. A servant came running with the message. "Shadwell has burned down! Your family is safe, Mr. Tom," he gasped. "Your furniture and books burned up. But we saved your fiddle!"

Tom raced back to Shadwell. Smoke filled the air. The ashes still glowed red. "I feel worst about losing my books," he said. "I must buy a new library."

With Shadwell destroyed, Tom was anxious to finish his new house. And he had another reason to hurry. He had fallen in love with a pretty young woman named Martha Wayles Skelton.

Martha was more than pretty. She was bright and interesting. Like Tom, Martha loved music. When she played the clavichord, Tom played his violin. They often sang together. Martha's hair shone in the soft candlelight. Tom bent close.

Tom and Martha were married on New Year's Day in 1772.

Martha loved Monticello as much as Tom did. She helped him plant the gardens. They rode together over the mountain trails.

Monticello, Tom's beautiful mountain-top home, was his childhood dream come true.

The family at Monticello was soon much larger. Tom's sister Martha and her six children came to live with him. Dabney Carr had died. He was buried under the big oak as Tom had promised.

The wide green lawn at Monticello was there for the children to play on. There was room in the large stable for several ponies and a small pony cart. The children were always happy to be with Tom. He taught the boys to hunt and fish. He showed the little girls flowers and animals.

The next year there was a new baby at Monticello. Tom and Martha had a little girl of their own. She was named Martha, but nicknamed Patsy.

The older children were delighted. They leaned over small Patsy's cradle. "No baby ever had *more* loving cousins," Tom said.

"Or a more adoring papa," Martha smiled.

## 5. Declaration of Independence

In the next years Tom was very busy at his law office. He worked hard. Life was happy at Monticello.

But the people in the American colonies were not happy with their government. The colonies still belonged to England, and she made most of the laws for the Americans. She had said the colonies could not sell their goods to any country except England. The English king made the colonies pay high taxes. Many Americans were angry.

Tom was angry too. He believed that countries should be fair, just as people should be fair. He thought England was making unfair laws.

There was a small group in Virginia which could make some of the rules and laws for the colony. It was called the House of Burgesses. Tom was elected to the House. The first law that he worked for was against slavery. He believed all people should be free.

In May 1774, the English governor closed the House of Burgesses. The leaders of Virginia voted to meet again anyhow.

Tom worked all one night on a message to the leaders. He said all people had the right to a good government that treated men fairly. When a government was unfair, as England was, people should break away from it. The people should start a new government.

He said all people should be part of the government. All people should vote. They should be free to speak and act as they felt right. They should be free to choose any religion they wanted.

Tom's speech was read to the meeting. Some did not agree with his ideas. But they said, "Tom Jefferson is a good writer. He can put words on paper that ring like a bell."

Far away in Philadelphia, in the colony of Pennsylvania, another group of men was meeting. It was the first Continental Congress. These men were leaders from all of the colonies. They knew the colonies might have to go to war against England.

In 1775 Tom was elected to the Continental Congress. He had to leave Martha and the children and travel many miles to Philadelphia.

"We are not separate colonies now," the men in Congress said. "We are a new *united* country. We must declare America free from England."

The State House in Philadelphia, where the first Continental Congress met.

Thomas Jefferson, author of the Declaration of Independence, and one of the first drafts of the document. Note the many changes made by Jefferson and others.

Congress wanted the words of the declaration to be written so that every member could sign them. A committee was formed to write the words. Thomas Jefferson and Benjamin Franklin were on the committee. Tom was thirty-three years old. Dr. Franklin was much older. Everyone had heard of him. He was a great American statesman. Tom thought Dr. Franklin should write the declaration.

"No," Dr. Franklin said, "you are the best writer, Tom. You must write for all of us."

Tom went to his room that night. He told his landlady, "I will be busy. Please bring me my meals, and keep visitors away."

Tom shut the door. He was alone. He laid out paper and sharpened his quill pens. He bent over his desk.

Late that night Tom got up from his chair. He had worked for hours. Only a few lines were written. He went to the window and looked down at the quiet square. "I would give the world and the moon to saddle a horse and ride for an hour," Tom thought. He sighed and went back to his desk.

Tom worked for eighteen days. He hardly slept. The weather was hot. Flies buzzed around Tom's head. He wrote page after page and threw them away. He crossed out words and wrote new words. He weighed each word as if it were gold.

Tom's landlady would peek through the door. She worried because Tom worked so hard. He looked even younger than he was, with his red hair and freckled face.

At last Tom finished. "I have done my best," he told Dr. Franklin. "It would have been easier to dig a ditch twenty times around the square than write these few pages." Franklin read the pages Tom had written. The others on the committee read them too. They changed some words, and then the declaration was read to Congress.

Tom sat quiet, listening. He heard the words he had worked so hard to write.

> . . . We hold these truths to be self-evident, that all men are created equal . . . with certain unalienable rights, that among these are life, liberty and the pursuit of happiness. . . . That these United Colonies are, and of right ought to be Free and Independent States. . . .

Congress voted for the Declaration of Independence on July 4, 1776. Later it was read to a cheering crowd in the square. The State House bell rang out. Afterward it was called the Liberty Bell in remembrance of the great day.

At the first celebration of independence, the new
Declaration was read to the cheering citizens of a
new nation.

Riders raced to carry the news to other cities. Everywhere people cheered. Church bells rang. Bonfires were lighted.

The Declaration lighted a bonfire in the whole world. It gave the world a new idea of a government where people would be free and equal. It would be a government where all people could vote for what they wanted.

Americans had already begun fighting *against* England. Now they would fight *for* the Declaration of Independence.

## 6. Ride for Liberty

Thomas Jefferson now had work to do in Virginia. The Declaration of Independence said that all men were born free and equal, but Thomas believed there must be new laws to make the words come true. He wanted to help write the laws.

Thomas wanted a law that would provide free schools for all children. The law was not passed. Thomas was not discouraged. "People are slow to accept new ideas," he said. "We must be patient."

He was pleased when his law for freedom of religion was passed.

Thomas was glad to be at Monticello again. Martha had been sick; now she was better.

There was a new baby in the nursery. Her name was Mary. The other children were happy to have Thomas at home. He built a schoolhouse for them, and he often came to hear their lessons. The children giggled when he tried to fold his long legs under a small desk.

After supper the family often sat around the fire. They played games or told stories. Then Thomas would let each of the children choose a book from his large library. Even the youngest ones pretended to read their books. They turned the pages and looked at the pictures. Thomas often looked up from his own book to see the circle of young faces in the firelight.

The next year Thomas Jefferson was elected governor of Virginia. It was a great honor, but it was a hard time to be governor. The war had gone on for four years. People were tired and discouraged. Virginia had sent soldiers to help General Washington in the North. They had sent food and money, even horses from their farms.

Now the British troops began to attack Virginia. There were only a few soldiers left at home to fight. People were frightened. "We elected Thomas Jefferson governor," they said. "He must save us now."

On Christmas day in 1780 Thomas and Martha were in Richmond, Virginia's new capital. The children had opened their presents. Suddenly a guard rushed in.

"British soldiers are coming," he said. "They want to capture every member of the government. You must escape."

Thomas acted quickly. He took his family to a friend's house across the river. Then Thomas turned his horse back toward Richmond. He wanted to help save the capital. His horse was worn out. It fell beside the road.

Thomas carried his saddle to the nearest farmhouse. "I must have a horse to get to Richmond," he said.

Thomas's face was dirty. His clothes were dusty. But the farmer knew him. "Governor, I have only one colt left," he said. "He has never been saddled. No one could ride him."

Thomas had ridden colts since he was a boy. "I will saddle your colt," he answered. "I will ride him."

The wild young horse did not have time to be frightened. Tom threw a saddle over his back and jumped on. At the edge of town Tom heard that the British had captured Richmond. They had set fire to the town.

Thomas worked night and day with others who had come to help. He found food for hungry people and shelter for families whose houses had been burned.

The British attacked Virginia again and again. They burned the crops of tobacco and wheat.

Thomas did his best to be a good governor. Still some people said Thomas should have defended Virginia better.

Thomas made a speech to the assembly. "I could not defend Virginia. She had sent her soldiers to fight in the North," he said. "We had only a few men left. But we fought our best."

When Thomas finished, the assembly cheered. They all voted that Thomas had been right.

Two years later the long war ended. The colonies had won their freedom from England.

## 7. Citizen of the World

Before the war was over Martha Jefferson was sick again. Thomas stopped his work to help take care of her, but she grew weaker. On a September day, when the woods were full of golden sunshine, Martha died.

At first Thomas felt as if his own life had ended. He locked himself in his room alone. He did not care whether the sun shone or whether his garden grew. He did not hear the birds sing. He was sad for his dear wife and their happy years together.

At last one morning there was a soft knock at Thomas's door. "Papa," his daughter Patsy called gently. "We are lonely without you. Please come back."

Thomas Jefferson served as American ambassador to France between 1785 and 1789. He is seen here as he appeared in the French capital during those years.

Thomas opened the door. He looked down at the ten-year-old girl. She had picked a little bunch of flowers for him. Thomas took her hand. "Let's go for a ride," he said.

They rode down a mountain path. Patsy was beside her father on her pony. At first Thomas did not speak. Then he remembered how Martha had loved the woods. He heard a mockingbird. He turned to Patsy. "It's good to be out again," Thomas said. "We must take Mary for a ride in the pony cart tomorrow."

Thomas went back to his work again. But he came home to his daughters as often as he could.

Two years later the government had a special job for Thomas. He was sent to France. He worked with the American ambassador, Benjamin Franklin. They would help build up trade between America and France. The two countries would sell each other crops and goods.

Mary was too young to travel. She would stay with her aunt. Patsy was twelve. She could go with her father. Their ship sailed on July 5, 1784.

Patsy learned French quickly. Her father wrote home, "Patsy chatters like a young French magpie. She makes friends with everyone. She is a fine ambassador herself!"

Thomas and Patsy were delighted to be in France. The country was beautiful. "French people are always smiling," Patsy told her father. Thomas wrote, "I do love these French people with all my heart."

Thomas lived in a house near Paris. "The rent is too high," he said. "But I pay it gladly for the garden. I cannot live happily without trees and flowers."

Thomas started work with Dr. Franklin. Often after a long day's work, Franklin asked Thomas to stay for supper. Thomas told him about his little elevator which brought up food from the kitchen. "Since it *waits* but never *speaks*, we call it a *dumbwaiter*," he said.

He described his desk chair that turned around. "I thought I would find it useful," Thomas said, "but the children are always spinning in it. They call it the 'whirlygig' chair."

Dr. Franklin was delighted. He was an inventor himself.

Patsy went to a convent school. Thomas came to see her every week. When Mary Jefferson was eight years old she came to France too.

At first Mary did not want to come to a strange country. She did not want to leave her friends at home. "I cannot help crying so please don't ask me to," she said. But Mary soon had new friends. She went to school with Patsy.

When Thomas came to visit them, Mary was already speaking French. "Everyone in school calls me

Thomas Jefferson's beloved Patsy. She is seen here as a young woman.

Maria," she told her father. "You must call me Maria too."

While Thomas was in France he hurt his right wrist. It did not heal completely. He learned to write with his left hand, but he could never play his violin again. "Now I can only listen to music," Thomas said.

Thomas traveled in France and Italy. He talked to farmers about their crops. He sent seeds home to Virginia. He bought new books for his library. He was interested in everything.

It was five years before Thomas and the girls returned to Monticello. It was a happy homecoming.

Their friends and servants came out to meet them as the carriage drove up the mountain.

A few months later there was a wedding at Monticello. Patsy, now a young lady, was marrying Thomas Randolph. The house was filled with guests. Patsy was a beautiful and happy bride; Maria was her bridesmaid. Thomas was proud of his daughters.

## 8. Mr. President

Thomas could not stay at Monticello long. General George Washington was now the first president of the United States. He made Thomas the first secretary of state. Thomas would advise the new president. He would help keep America friendly with other countries.

Thomas also helped plan the city of Washington. It would be the new capital. Later Thomas was elected vice-president.

There were many arguments in the new government. Some leaders did not really believe that all people are equal. They wanted a "ruling class." They said only people who owned land should vote. They also wanted to treat the president like a king.

Thomas argued with these leaders. "A president should not be a king. He should be called 'Mister.' We do not need classes. *All* Americans are equal and should be able to vote."

Some men called Thomas a dreamer. "Jefferson believes all people are born wise," they said.

But Thomas was not a dreamer. He knew people must be educated to be good citizens. That is why he wanted free schools and libraries for all Americans.

More and more people believed Jefferson was right. They wanted him to lead the country. In 1800 they elected Thomas Jefferson the third president of the United States.

He left for Washington in February. The woods were bare and wintry. Patsy and her husband would live at Monticello while Thomas was away. The grandchildren raced after Jefferson's carriage. Little Peter called, "Be a good president, grandpa!"

The new "President's House" in Washington was not finished. Later it would be the beautiful White House. But now the rooms were bare. There was not enough furniture. Thomas sent this riddle home to his grandchildren:

Question: What does the President stand for?

Answer: Because he has no chair to sit down on.

Thomas sent home to Monticello for more furniture. "Be sure to send my whirlygig chair," he said. "At

A view of the Capitol of the United States before 1814. The first of these towering poplars was planted at Jefferson's direction.

least it will give me a little exercise. I ride for an hour each morning. The rest of the day I am saddled to my desk. But I am not here to enjoy myself, I am here to work. And there is plenty of work!"

Jefferson had promised there would be no more secrets in the government. Now he told the people everything the government was doing. The government money was counted carefully. He made taxes lower.

The president liked to walk about Washington in his old brown coat. Patsy and Maria thought he should dress up more. "You look like a farmer, papa," they fussed.

"I am a farmer," Jefferson smiled.

People on the street often stopped to shake hands with the president.

Before long the president had a problem. A huge tract of land between the Mississippi River and the Rocky Mountains, called the Louisiana Territory, belonged to Spain. Jefferson learned, to his dismay, that Spain had secretly given Louisiana to France.

The city of New Orleans, a large seaport at the mouth of the Mississippi River, was important to the United States. Jefferson feared that France might close the port of New Orleans to American trade. He also felt that it was dangerous to have a strong foreign country so close to the United States.

Jefferson sent agents to Paris to ask France to sell New Orleans to the United States. The president waited anxiously for France to answer.

One morning in 1803 the president was up at daylight. A cold October wind rattled the windows. He pulled on a woolen sweater. His desk was piled high with work.

Later his servant Jupiter brought his breakfast. "I have a surprise for you, Mr. President," Jupiter said. He put a cage with a small gray bird on the desk.

The president stared; then he smiled. The tired

The United States flag replaced the French flag, and the Louisiana Territory became a part of the young nation. The purchase was thought by many to be Jefferson's finest accomplishment as president.

look left his face. "A mockingbird!" he said. "It must have come from Virginia." He put a finger gently between the cage bars. He held out a crumb of bread to coax the bird closer.

The new pet was the president's joy. The cage door was often open. The bird sat on the president's shoulder and sang in his ear.

Finally the great news arrived. France was willing to sell not only New Orleans, but all of the Louisiana Territory for the sum of fifteen million dollars! With the Louisiana Purchase, the United States had almost doubled in size. Jefferson was elated. He hoped some day the United States would reach all the way to the Pacific Ocean. With this purpose in mind, he sent two young explorers, Lewis and Clark, to the Northwest. He studied the maps they brought back.

At the end of his first term, President Jefferson was so popular that the people elected him to a second term.

## 9. Embargo

The president had never forgotten his friendship with the Indians. He knew many Indian tribes had been pushed off their land by white settlers. Some had no homes or food. "We must treat the Indians fairly," Jefferson said. "We must give them new land

and teach them to be farmers. Their children must have schools."

Soon the president was faced with new trouble abroad. England and France were fighting. They both needed extra ships and more sailors. They began stopping American ships at sea and kidnapping American sailors. Many people thought the United States should declare war.

Jefferson was discouraged. He had always believed countries could be friendly. He did not think America should declare war.

Jefferson thought of a plan for peace. "We will keep our ships at home and forbid them to trade with foreign countries," he said. "When other countries find they cannot trade with America they won't stop our ships and capture our sailors."

Congress passed the Embargo Act. It kept America from sending goods to other countries.

Many businessmen opposed the embargo. People who owned factories could not sell their goods abroad. Farmers could not sell all their crops. Business was bad, and many people had no work. They were angry with the president.

Jefferson did not blame people for being upset when business was bad. Still he did not change his mind. "The embargo loses us trade," he said, "but it is better than war."

A visit from Patsy and her family cheered the president. The children rushed to hug him. "Can we play in your whirlygig chair, grandpa?" they shouted. "Who can have the first turn?"

Congress repealed the Embargo Act and substituted another law. It was not much more successful than the Embargo Act had been. The trouble with England continued, and, finally, in the next president's term the United States and England fought the War of 1812.

In the last days of Jefferson's administration, he signed an important law forbidding traders from bringing any more slaves to America. Jefferson had worked hard for the law. He knew it would help end slavery.

Jefferson's years as president were almost over. He was pleased when his friend James Madison was elected as the new president.

Even though the embargo had been unpopular, people felt that Jefferson had been a good president. He had made America bigger and stronger. He had helped people understand the government. He had tried to make the people part of the government.

## 10. Voices of the Future

Patsy came to Washington to help her father move. She found the president with piles of books and papers ready to pack. One special box held Jefferson's notes on the Indian languages.

Patsy's blue cloak matched her eyes. Her cheeks were glowing. "You look like a breath of fresh Virginia air," her father smiled. "And far too young and pretty to be the mother of so many children. How are the young rapscallions?"

"All waiting for you to be home again," Patsy answered. "And very proud of their 'President Grandpapa.'"

On the trip home thieves stole some of the president's things. They took the box with his Indian notes. It was never found again.

Jefferson was sad. "I studied for years to make the notes," he said. "I wanted to write a book about the Indian languages. Now it is too late to start again."

But Jefferson found other work to do. He ran the farm. He wrote about music and science and education and government. He advised the new presidents. He never stopped working for the things he believed in.

Now he had time to read his books. He rode his horse Eagle every day. He wrote, "My crops do very well, including grandchildren."

Patsy and her family stayed at Monticello. There were eleven children. The schoolhouse at Monticello was full again.

Jefferson was asked to help plan a new college in Charlottesville. It would be the University of Virginia. Jefferson was delighted. Soon his desk was covered with drawings of the college buildings.

While the college was being built Jefferson watched every brick go into place. When he could not go to Charlottesville, he sat on his porch and watched through his telescope.

Jefferson lived to be eighty-three. He died on the Fourth of July in 1826. He was buried near

An early engraving of the University of Virginia

the big oak tree he and Dabney had chosen. The stone on his grave says: "Author of the Declaration of Independence. . . ."

Today the beautiful house at Monticello is kept as a museum by the state of Virginia. Many people go there to visit. They see the furniture Jefferson used, and they walk through the gardens he and Martha planted.

Thomas Jefferson would be pleased to have so many visitors. He always welcomed company. He would be glad to hear children's voices in his house. He called them "the voices of the future. . . . "

This portrait shows the brilliant diplomat and able third president standing in front of the Natural Bridge of his native Virginia.

# Mr. Jefferson's Washington

### by Esther M. Douty

From *Mr. Jefferson's Washington* by Esther M. Douty (Champaign, Illinois: 1970). Reprinted by permission of the author.

## "Government's In!"

The second of June 1800 was a fine cool day in Washington. At Lear's Wharf, where the sparkling Potomac merged with the clear waters of Rock Creek, a line of wagons and carts awaited the arrival of the sloops from Philadelphia.

Among them was the cart belonging to the Hines brothers, Christian, Matthew, and Frederick. Chris, now nineteen, sat quietly talking with fifteen-year-old Matt. Twelve-year-old Fred kept jumping out of the cart and running to the river to watch for the approaching sails.

Suddenly a shout went up from the men on the wharf. "There they are. Government's in."

"Government's in." It was a happy shout. Many of

the 3,200 people in the tiny city had been waiting for a long time to hear it. Their chief regret was that George Washington could not share this joyous occasion with them. He had died six months earlier.

When the sloops "bringing the government" tied up at the wharf, Fred Hines half-expected to see President John Adams, or at least Vice-President Jefferson, step from the decks; but only stacks of desks and chairs, and boxes of books and papers met his eye.

There was no place to put much of the furniture and boxes. Philadelphia had had many spacious buildings to serve as government offices. In Washington, after eight years of effort, only the Treasury Building, near the President's House, was ready for occupancy. The State Department had to squeeze in with the Treasury. The War and Post Office departments were placed in private houses rented by the government.

Unloading was slow, but finally the Hines brothers' cart creaked away with boxes of records marked "War Department."

By June 15, 1800, the entire United States government, including the 131 government employees and their families, had been transferred to Washington. The newcomers had a hard time finding places to live, for the wilderness city had few dwellings of any kind for anyone.

The tiny new Federal City was surrounded by the lush countryside of Maryland and Virginia.

From Capitol Hill the new residents had a fine view of the whole Territory of Columbia. Forests, meadows with wild flowers, orchards, corn, wheat, and tobacco crops still covered much of the land marked for streets, although wide paths cut through the woods showed where the most important thoroughfares were to be.

Even though the streets themselves were not there, newcomers quickly learned the plans of Washington's streets. The four sections of the city—north, south, east, and west—began at the Capitol. The most important streets also began there. Streets running east

147

and west were named for letters of the alphabet. Streets running north and south were numbered, beginning with First Street.

Broad avenues, named for the states, had also been planned. These too radiated from the Capitol, like rays from the sun. The finest of them all was to be Pennsylvania Avenue, which ran from the President's House to the Capitol. But simple as the plan was, it would be years before people would use the names of the streets. Instead they would say, "a few paces from the Capitol," or "on the high ground near the President's House," or "forty rods east of the War Office."

Although everyone admired Washington's natural beauty, a closer look at the village-city brought disappointment, even shock, to many persons who moved there during the summer and fall of 1800. One congressman lamented that the "whole federal city, as connected with the Capitol, consisted of seven or eight boarding houses, one tailor, one shoemaker, one printer, a washerwoman, a grocery shop, a pamphlets and stationer shop, a small drygoods shop, and an oyster house."

The secretary of the treasury said, "There are but few houses at any one place, and most of them are small, miserable huts." A senator complained that the capital was "a hateful place, with the feeling that creeping things had possession of the place, and foxes looked out of windows."

A diplomat who found a snake two feet long in his house cried, "My God, what have I done to be condemned to reside in such a city?"

This diplomat, like most of the other residents, also worried about his health, for Washington was a sickly city. In the summer the flies were everywhere. They swarmed from the stables and from the manure lying near almost every home. They feasted on the garbage the householders dumped into the streets. They buzzed around the pigs scavenging in that garbage. Wherever the flies went they carried dysentery and typhoid fever.

The swamps near the river and the pools of stagnant water in the excavations for buildings also accounted for much of the capital's sickness. Here, mosquitos bred by the millions. With the mosquitos came yellow fever and malaria.

Furthermore, the new capital was constantly threatened by fire, and the citizens had only the most primitive means of fighting it. At the shout of "fire," people would fill leather buckets at the nearest river, creek, or spring, and dash to the blaze. Here they handed the buckets to a line of fire fighters who tossed the water on the flames and then passed the buckets back to be filled again.

John Adams was the first president to live in the new Federal City.

Scarcely had the War Department moved into its quarters in November 1800, when the house burned down. Most of the Revolutionary War records were lost. One freezing night two months later, flames again licked toward the sky near the President's House.

Mr. Hines and the older boys grabbed the buckets that always stood beside their back door and raced toward the blaze. This time the Treasury Department was in flames. By the light of the fire, Chris Hines could see President Adams in the line of fire fighters. He worked as hard as any of the men until the fire was out.

150

## Congress Is at Home

The whole Hines family planned to attend the first meeting of Congress in Washington, which was to take place on November 21, 1800. But the day before, it snowed so hard that no one could tell where the road up Capitol Hill was supposed to be. Congress had to postpone its first meeting in the Capitol until the twenty-second. This was a cold and cloudy Saturday.

The family left early for the Capitol, where only the north wing was finished. They decided it would be safer to walk. Their cart might get caught on a stump or turn over in some hole hidden by the snow.

When they reached the Capitol, they found the Senate chamber already crowded, not only with senators and congressmen but with fashionably dressed ladies who had come to watch the ceremony. The Hines family was among the many crowded into the galleries. Fred was glad he was upstairs where he could get a good look at the legislators—the 44 congressmen and 13 senators who had managed to be present.

While he waited for President John Adams to appear, Fred looked around the Senate chamber. Each senator had a fine chair of red leather to sit in. If he got cold, the senator could move to the back of the room and sit on one of the couches placed around two huge fireplaces blazing with great fires.

At noon a hush fell over the chamber. The Hines boys leaned over the railing. They could just see John Adams, second president of the United States. He was short and pudgy, and his round cheeks glowed red. He wore a formal black coat and knee breeches. Speaking in a clear, high-pitched voice, President Adams congratulated the people of the United States on the seating of Congress in its permanent home.

The president's address was only part of the ceremony for the opening of Congress. After the address, the entire Congress was supposed to call upon the president at his official home. But now, as the legislators streamed out of the Capitol, they stared down in dismay at the half-frozen swamp they would have to cross to reach the President's House. The members had not faced that problem in getting to the Capitol because almost all of them were staying in boardinghouses or at the one hotel on Capitol Hill. Walking to the Capitol, even through the slush, had not been difficult.

"The capital of our nation, and not a hackney coach to be had," grumbled a senator from Pennsylvania, as he looked around for some conveyance to take him to the President's House.

Then to everyone's pleased surprise, a line of hackney coaches did appear, rolling in from the northeast.

This wing of the new Capitol was the first to be completed. It served for a time as the home of the Senate, the House, and the Supreme Court.

Someone had had the foresight to send to Baltimore, forty miles away, for them. The legislators climbed into the vehicles. With the sergeant-at-arms on horseback and carrying the mace (the symbol of authority), the coaches wound cautiously down the slippery hill and around the treacherous swamp to the President's House.

Many of the congressmen who visited President and Mrs. Adams were shocked by the damp, chilly, unfinished mansion they lived in. Many of the walls were still unplastered. There was no stairway to the second floor, and wooden shelves served as makeshift mantelpieces. Nor were there any bells to summon the servants who would be necessary "to assist in this great castle."

Despite the congressmen's displeasure, the condition of the president's home was slow to improve. Not enough craftsmen could be found to work on the President's House or on the Capitol, and the Capitol was considered more important. For over two years after the Adams term of office ended, the President's House remained "fenceless, stairless, bell-less, and at times almost fireless in the cold of winter."

With so many difficulties to overcome in building the Federal City, it was not surprising that people whispered that the government would not remain long in Washington.

## Boardinghouse Hill

Matt Hines had sharp eyes. They were especially sharp when it came to picking out interesting items from the tiny print of Washington's newspaper, the *National Intelligencer*. On Friday, November 28, 1800, he read: "Last evening, arrived in Washington, Thomas Jefferson, Vice-President of the United States, and took up his lodgings in Messr's Conrad and McMunn's Apartments."

"Apartments" was simply another way of saying "boardinghouse." In the new capital, almost every congressman and senator lived in one of them. With so few houses and hotels built, they had no other choice.

In 1801 there were eight boardinghouses, all clustered near the Capitol. Within these boardinghouses the legislators lived uncomfortably. Few had rooms or even beds to themselves. Sometimes five and six House members shared a room. Even senators slept two or more to a bed.

They were summoned to the dining hall by the breakfast or dinner bell "like scholars in colleges or monks in a monastery." "Messmates," as the boarders were called, took their meals seated at one long table called the "ordinary." They were served by the proprietor on plates handed down from the head of the table. All boarders were placed on an equal footing, no matter what their rank.

Even Vice-President Jefferson, although he did have a separate room in which to receive visitors, "lived on a perfect equality with his fellow boarders and ate at a common table. Even here," wrote a friend, "so far from taking precedence of the other members of Congress, he always placed himself at the lowest end of the table." Mrs. Brown, the wife of the senator from Kentucky, suggested that a seat should be offered him at the upper end, near the fire, if not on account of his rank as vice-president, at least as the oldest man in the company. (He was fifty-seven.)

> But the idea was rejected, and he occupied during the whole winter the lowest and coldest seat at a long table at which more than thirty sat down.

In the evening after dinner, the congressmen would gather in the common room, or parlor. Manners were informal. Usually there were no ladies around, and the congressmen threw off their coats and even removed their shoes. They received their guests in a room that was always noisy and crowded. Those who had no guests would play cards, tell tales, or talk over the events of the day, which were related to politics.

A corner of E Street in 1817. Washington still looked like a country town during the early 1800s.

Seldom, unless there was a full moon, did a congressman venture from his boardinghouse at night. The city had no lighting except for two lanterns placed on the bridges at M Street, and a third tied to a tree where Capitol Hill ran into Pennsylvania Avenue. Walking or riding in the blackness was dangerous. One might fall into a deep mudhole, injure oneself against the stump of a newly cut tree, scratch one's face on the bramble bushes which were everywhere, or get lost and wander about until dawn.

The boardinghouse groups, or Congressional Messes, were nearly always made up of men from the same state, or at least from the same region. The typical boardinghouse group was a party of Southerners or of New Englanders, or perhaps a "sett" of Pennsylvanians, New Yorkers, and Jerseymen. In Mr. Jefferson's Washington, congressmen felt most comfortable with the kind of people they had known back home. They seldom visited with members of other Congressional Messes.

Some people thought that, since congressmen had no offices, they used their boardinghouse parlors to plan political strategy and so wanted no outsiders present. It was certainly true that congressmen who lived together usually voted as a group.

Even though the congressmen made good friends among their fellow boarders, they missed having a home and being part of a family. If they knew some-one fortunate enough to have a family and a house in the city, they might wear out their welcome with frequent "drop-ins" for dinner or for tea. Washington wives grew accustomed to having congressmen appear at their homes even before the family had breakfasted.

Often, as the sessions wore on, the legislators in their boardinghouses became bored and irritable with one another. "The company is good enough, but it is always the same," a Pennsylvania congressman com-plained mildly. "I had rather now and then see other persons."

One Virginia congressman was not so mild. In a burst of anger at the dinner table, he dashed a glass of wine in the face of another congressman. In return, this boarder flung a decanter at the Virginian's head. Soon, as the other legislators fled, the room was littered with shattered glass. Scuffling in the boardinghouses was common, but so long as the fights did not lead to duels, few people appeared to take the brawling seriously.

The six Supreme Court justices also lived on Boardinghouse Hill. During the two months when the court was in session, they walked to the small room on the ground floor of the Capitol that served as the Supreme Court.

## Mr. Jefferson Becomes President

On the morning of March 4, 1801, one boarder at Conrad and McMunn's arose very early and glanced out of his bedroom window toward the Potomac River. A whitish mist hovered above the water, but he could see a hint of blue sky and pale gold sun. How good, the boarder thought, to have a sunny day when he, Thomas Jefferson, was to be inaugurated as third president of the United States.

The Hines boys had also risen very early. They wanted to get to the Capitol early enough to have a chance of getting into the Senate chamber to watch the inauguration ceremony. But already crowds were pouring into the capital. The roads from Maryland and Virginia were packed with wagons, carriages, people on horseback, and pedestrians, all heading for the Capitol.

By the time the brothers reached Capitol Hill, a throng of happy people had gathered outside of Mr. Jefferson's boardinghouse, cheering him and singing his campaign song, "Jefferson and Liberty." Everybody in Washington, from highest official to humblest apprentice, appeared to have taken the day off.

Shortly before noon, Mr. Jefferson, accompanied by several officials and friends, stepped from his boardinghouse and headed across a muddy field toward the Capitol.

"Mr. Jefferson's dress was as usual," said the *Intelligencer*, "that of a plain man without any distinctive badge of office." Actually, the Hines boys noticed, he was wearing a blue coat with brass buttons, green homespun breeches, gray woolen stockings, a gray waistcoat, and shoes tied with leather strings.

As he made his way through the throng, a joyful shout arose, "Three cheers for Jefferson, the friend of the people." Guns boomed as he entered the Capitol.

The Senate chamber was small. Matt and Fred were not lucky enough to crowd inside to watch the inauguration ceremony. Instead they waited until the ceremony was over, and the tall, graceful figure of the new president emerged from the Capitol. Again the guns boomed in salute. The boys then joined the crowd of well-wishers who walked with Mr. Jefferson back across the muddy field to his boardinghouse.

That evening the new president held open house. His reception room at Conrad and McMunn's was packed with men and women of all walks of life. The entire diplomatic corps—the men representing Britain, France, Spain, and Denmark—was present. They unenthusiastically rubbed elbows and drank wine with the carpenters, the bricklayers, and the stonecutters whom Mr. Jefferson had cordially invited to the party.

The President's House changed slowly over the years. This drawing by Benjamin Latrobe shows changes he proposed to Thomas Jefferson.

Two weeks later Mr. Jefferson moved into the President's House. He moved in alone because he had no family to share it with him. His wife and four of his six children had died years before. His two married daughters lived in Virginia with their own families.

The new president found his house "big enough for two emperors, one Pope, and the Grand Lama."

Still, he tried to make himself as comfortable as possible in the unfinished mansion. He was the second president to occupy the great house which the nation had provided for its chief executive. It was clear to see that the government was settling in.

Mr. Jefferson felt sure that the new capital would be a success after all!

# Index

## A

Adams, John, 146, 150 (pic), 151, 152, 154
Allegheny River, 65
American Philosophical Society, 51
Articles of Confederation, 41, 43

## B

Bache, Benjamin (grandson of Benjamin Franklin), 32, 33, 35, 38, 40, 41
Bache, Sally (daughter of Benjamin Franklin), 21, 29, 30, 32, 36
Bache, William (grandson of Benjamin Franklin), 32, 33
Bache, William, 32
Ballooning, 39 (pic), 40
Boardinghouse Hill, 157, 158–159
Boston, 10, 70, 71
Braddock, Edward, 66

## C

Carr, Dabney, 111, 112, 114, 117
Cherokee Indians, 107
Chief Ontassette, 107, 110
Collins, John, 15, 18
Congress, 85, 88, 91, 139, 151
Constitutional Convention, 43, 46, 54, 55, 84
Constitution of the United States, 43, 84, 85
Continental Congress, 33, 54, 70, 72, 119, 122
Cornwallis, Charles, 81
Custis, George, 93
Custis, Jackie (stepson of George Washington), 68, 69
Custis, Martha. See Washington, Martha
Custis, Nelly, 93

Custis, Patsy (stepdaughter of George Washington), 68, 69

## D

Declaration of Independence, 33, 72, 120 (pic), 121, 122, 123 (pic), 124
Dinwiddie, Robert, 62, 63, 65, 66

## E

Embargo Act, 138, 139
England, 33, 63, 66, 68, 77, 90–91, 118, 138

## F

Fairfax, Sally, 62
Forbes, John, 68
Fort Necessity, 66
France, 33, 37, 63, 66, 68, 79–80, 81, 90, 129, 135, 138
Franklin, Benjamin, 8 (pic), 36 (pic), 42 (pic)
  as apprentice, 13, 14, 15, 16, 18
  as author, 15–16
  birth of, 11
  childhood of, 10, 11
  and Constitutional Convention, 43, 84
  death of, 43
  and Declaration of Independence, 33, 121, 122
  education of, 11
  and experiments with electricity, 26–27, 28 (pic)
  in England, 29, 30, 31 (pic), 32
  and father, 11, 13
  as fireman, 25 (pic)
  in France, 33, 35, 37, 38, 39, 40, 50, 129, 130
  honors to, 29, 36
  illnesses of, 36, 49